The New Leader's Playbook

Volume I - 2011

George Bradt's Forbes Articles

Examples of leadership for you to follow.

George Bradt

GHP Press

Copyright © 2019 by George Bradt. All rights reserved.

No part of this publication may be reproduced, stored in a retrieval system, or transmitted in any form or by any means, electronic, mechanical, photocopying, recording, scanning, or otherwise, except as permitted under Section 107 or 108 of the 1976 United States Copyright Act, without either the prior written permission of the Publisher, or authorization through payment of the appropriate per-copy fee to the Copyright Clearance Center, 222 Rosewood Drive, Danvers, MA 01923, (978) 750-8400, fax (978) 646-8600, or on the web at www.copyright.com. Requests to the publisher for permission should be addressed to gbradt@primegenesis.com at GHP Press.

Limit of Liability/Disclaimer of Warranty: While the publisher and author have used their best efforts in preparing this book, they make no representations or warranties with the respect to the accuracy or completeness of the contents of this book and specifically disclaim any implied warranties of merchantability or fitness for a particular purpose. No warranty may be created or extended by sales representatives or written sales materials. The advice and strategies contained herein may not be suitable for your situation. You should consult with a professional where appropriate. Neither the publisher nor the author shall be liable for damages arising herefrom.

This is a compilation of the articles I published on Forbes.com in 2011.
The page readership counts were through December, 2019.

In general, I focus on executive onboarding and leading through points of
inflection to accelerate transitions, leveraging my own senior line
management and consulting experience, as well as my books including
"The New Leader's 100-Day Action Plan."

After I'd been contributing to Forbes for two months, I went in to meet
the Leadership editor at the time, Fred Allen. He told me that he liked my
articles, but bad news would get me more readers. I told him that he had a
whole range of contributors, most of which could talk about bad news. I
choose to focus on good news and examples of leadership for others to
follow.

So, if you're looking for bad news, look elsewhere. The vast majority of
articles in The New Leader's Playbook highlight things people do well,
leadership worth following and emulating. Read and heed.

George Bradt

Articles:

13 views Jan 20, 2011, 04:10pm

What Daley Must Do First As Obama's Chief Of Staff

First impressions count--especially at 1600 Pennsylvania Ave. As William Daley moves into his new role as White House chief of staff, all eyes will be on him. The pressure he will experience to perform quickly and effectively will be significant, especially in his first few days and weeks. It will be no less than he faced as Midwest chairman of JPMorgan Chase , responsible for overseeing post-merger operations.

To tackle the responsibilities of his new role and ensure that better results are delivered faster, he will have to act quickly. It will be critical for him to get a head start, ensure clear communication and rebuild his team. And those are steps useful not only for Daley in his new position but for all recently appointed business leaders in corporate America.

To make the most of the very short window between an announcement and a formal start, leaders must always quickly discern what matters, who matters and what to communicate--and in what priority.

One of the most important things leaders must do early is clarify and establish their organization's vision and values. In his new role Daley has a rare opportunity to help evolve the implementation of Obama's vision, values and priorities to fit the new political landscape. He should get in sync with Obama and then articulate exactly what is now expected of the staff in terms of behaviors, relationships, attitudes, values and work environment.

As chief of staff Daley will have relationships with more people in more organizations than most of us can comprehend. He must discern which of those people are going to be most important and reach out to them immediately--especially those who will soon encounter collaboration and negotiation instead of the aggressive and adversarial approach sometimes taken by Daley's predecessor, Rahm Emanuel.

Establishing those relationships sends that collaborative message in a way that would be difficult to do later. Preparation breeds confidence. The more business leaders can prepare and jump-start their learning and relationships in advance, the better.

Furthermore, Daley absolutely must get clear on Obama's and his own message and communication points immediately, then drive that message home through his staff.

There are going to be some who "get it," buy into it and support it, some who don't buy into it and who fight the change, and some who watch to see how things play out. Daley needs to empower those who "get it" and turn them into advocates, move some of the watchers into the supporter category, and get the ones fighting any change out of the way. The stakes are too high and the time is too short to put up with internal politicking.

It's important to remember that he will be judged initially not by what he says, but by what he does--and by whether that is in line with who he really is.

Finally, he must build the team. It is a team that has a number of new players beyond Daley. He needs to reform this team under the ultimate leadership of President Obama. There are steps commonly used in executive transitions that certainly apply here:

- Get people aligned around the new imperative, what the administration is determined to accomplish over the next two years.
- Set milestones, so everyone knows what must get done by whom, by when.
- Identify some early wins to build back momentum.
- Sort out people's roles to make sure the right people are focused on the right things with the right support (and the wrong people go off to do other things).
- Manage communication throughout.

These basic concepts apply to complex transitions in the private sector as well. It's always important to take a hard look at an organization's situation and culture to understand both its need for change and its openness to change. In almost every case, the executive leading the transition will be better off if he or she can get a head start, manage the message and build the team--fast.

9,456 views Feb 10, 2011, 11:17

Promoted From Within – Thoughts for Google's New CEO Larry Page

Image via Wikipedia

In general, when leaders are promoted from within, they need to keep in mind that they cannot control the context, cannot make a clean break, and have no honeymoon.

Given these, they need to manage the context they inherit as much as possible, take control of their own transition, and accelerate team progress after they start.

For Larry Page moving into the CEO role at Google, this means starting now to secure the resources and support he will need, deciding what parts of Eric Schmidt's legacy he will keep and what parts he will change, and evolving the stated and de facto strategies as appropriate.

Where one of the main transition management challenges for someone joining a new company is positioning themselves, the challenge for people like Larry, getting promoted from within, is repositioning themselves. Larry is not going to change who he is and his history with his colleagues. He's not going to change his strengths. But he can change his behaviors, how he relates to others, his attitude, and the work environment he creates, including which strengths he leverages first.

Secure needed resources and support

Most of us are unbalanced. We are relatively stronger in some areas than in others. No one is suggesting that Larry is going to be a better CEO than

Eric was. No one is suggesting that Eric was a better CEO than Larry was the first time or than Larry is going to be this time around. The choice made ten years ago was based on Eric's relative strengths being more important for that stage of growth. The choice being made now is based on Larry's strengths being more important for the next stage of growth.

PrimeGenesis partner Rob Gregory says that CEOs own three core processes: strategic, operational, and organizational. Larry's relative strengths are in the strategic area, continually re-figuring where Google should place future product bets. He is relatively less strong on the organizational side, and perhaps even less on the operational side. Google needs Larry to drive that strategic product area even more than he has. Google also needs the organization and operations to be managed well.

Larry is not going to take crash courses to build his strengths in organizational development and operations between now and April 1. What he can do is make sure he's got the resources and support lined up to compensate for his relative lack of strengths in these areas. Since his profile is different than Eric's, this probably means moving people with different strengths to different positions. Those with strengths complementary to Larry's need to play larger roles going forward than they did before. Larry needs to get these moves in process well before April 1.

Continuity and Change

In many ways, Larry went live in his new role the moment he was announced. While Eric is still running the day-to-day business, no one is going to make any decisions about anything that's going to impact anything beyond April 1 without checking with Larry. They don't want to risk his reversing decisions they make now as soon as he takes over.

Uncertainty is crippling. Not knowing what's happening, who's in, who's out, or in what direction we are going is a major cause of stress. Since stress is cumulative, the sooner Larry can explain to people what is going to stay the same and what is going to change, the sooner people can settle into their new reality. The sooner people know the general direction of things to come, the sooner they can stop going to Larry with every decision, and the more nimble Google will be. This is why Larry needs to publish the new direction sooner rather than later, managing communication to inspire and enable Google's people.

Evolving the Stated and De Facto Strategies

People joining from the outside have some small grace period during which they can ask "dumb" questions. Not so for someone promoted from within - and certainly not so for co-founder and returning CEO Larry Page. He will be expected to hit the ground at a full gallop and accelerate from there.

This means he cannot shut down, rethink, and re-start the core strategic, operational, and organizational processes. Instead, his should evolve them on the fly, starting with the strategies. a) Strategies inform everything else. b) This is where his own strengths lie. c) He can get started here now, not waiting until April 1, and then evolve the operational and organizational processes after that. Thus, this is where he can find his early wins.

Implications for You

General advice is generally useless – unless you can apply it to your own situation. When you're getting promoted from within, look hard at:

1. Preparing in advance, especially around securing the resources and support you'll need going forward.
2. Taking control of your own transition, especially around deciding what to keep the same and what to change.
3. Accelerating team progress after your start by evolving the strategies first, and then operations and organization.

The New Leader's Playbook

This is a good example of step 1 of The New Leader's Playbook, **Position Yourself for Success**

Start by connecting your values and goals, strengths and communication. Know yourself. Know your audience. Know and deliver your message in your own voice. Leadership is personal. Your message is the key that unlocks personal connections. The greater the congruence between your own values, attitudes, behaviors, the environment you create, and the way you relate to other individuals, the stronger those connections will be. This is why the best messages aren't crafted; they emerge. Great leaders live their messages not because they can, but because they must. As Martin Luther said at the Diet of Worms in 1521, "Here I stand, I can do no other."

1,164 views Feb 16, 2011, 11:27 am

A Shocking Approach by New UK Prime Minister David Cameron

Image by World Economic Forum via Flickr

Whether or not you agree with the direction the United Kingdom's new Prime Minister, David Cameron, is taking the country, there can be no doubt about his sense of urgency and the consistency of his direction.

The manner in which he has shocked the UK's political system serves as an excellent example of one way in which a new business leader can engage the culture he or she is going to dictate and lead.

Cameron's Transition Management

During the campaign, Mr. Cameron was unapologetically clear about what he had in mind, talking about how he "would get to grips with our debt and our deficit that is hanging over our economy like a black cloud," with an "emergency budget" (From Cameron's 24-April-2010 campaign speech).

He reiterated the point as soon as he took over. "I think the service our country needs right now is to face up to our really big challenges, to confront our problems, to take difficult decisions, to lead people through those difficult decisions, so that together we can reach better times ahead" (From Cameron's 1-May-2010 speech on taking over as Prime Minister).

Then, as promised, he and his team brought forward a particularly austere budget and pushed it through Parliament. This had painful budget cuts across the board including the elimination of 490,000 government jobs.

And he has stuck with his guns. "I won't hide from people that this is going to be a difficult year but I think we just have to keep on explaining... that if you don't deal with your debt and your deficit, you can end up like Greece or Ireland - in a real mess. We mustn't do that, so we have to go through this difficult year" (From Cameron's 31-January, 2011 interview with BBC1).

Application for New Business Leaders

Business Leaders should be careful about how they engage with the organization's existing business context and culture. They must examine the need for change and the readiness for change, to help them decide whether to assimilate in, converge and evolve in (fast or slow), or shock the organization.

David Cameron's actions are a good example of shocking a system that needed to be shocked. The optimal choice depends on the combination of the need for change and the organization's readiness for change:

- **Assimilating** works when there is a low need and high readiness for change. When the need to change arises, the organization is ready to step up.
- **Converging and evolving slowly** works when there is a low need and low readiness for change. The new leader has time to converge into the culture and then work from the inside to help it get ready to change over time.
- **Converging and evolving quickly** works when there is a high need and a high readiness for change. The new leader needs to converge quickly so he or she can evolve with the organization or it will leave him or her behind as it changes.
- **Shocking** is appropriate for situations where there is a high need and a low readiness for change. The organization can't see it, but it must change, urgently.

The Larger Implications

In this case, the changes in the world were leaving the United Kingdom behind. There was a real risk of its financial situation going the way of Greece or Ireland. Mr. Cameron seems to have chosen wisely in shocking the system and has implemented at least the early steps well.

In the United Kingdom's government, some of the most intractable players
are found in the civil service. Long-tenured members there have seen
governments come and go and they're still there. For many, their preferred
method of dealing with government change is to keep their heads down
and not make waves, knowing that if they can hide long enough they can
survive almost any government.

Mr. Cameron seems to have done a good job of mapping and moving
some of the key players as well. He figured out who were going to be the
early supporters of the change and enrolled them as champions of the
change. He changed the balance of consequences for some of those
watching from the sidelines to encourage them to jump on the bandwagon
sooner rather than later. And, he moved some of his detractors out of the
way quickly.

Remember that every organization has its own long-tenured civil servants.
It's not necessary to convince all of them to support the change you're
making, just make sure they don't derail the change by what they say or do,
or don't say or don't do. Change the balance of consequences to
discourage passive-aggressive resistance.

This is a good example of step 2 of The New Leader's Playbook, **Choose
How To Engage the Context and Culture**

Context is a function of the business environment, organizational history
and recent business performance, informing the relative importance and
urgency of change. Culture underpins "the way we do things here" and is
made up of Behaviors, Relationships, Attitudes, Values, and the
Environment feeding into readiness for change. Crossing context and
culture helps you decide whether to Assimilate, Converge and Evolve (fast
or slow), or Shock. Choose your way. Then map contributors, detractors,
and convincible watchers so you can move each of them one step by
altering their balance of consequences.

13,463 views Feb 23, 2011, 12:03pm

Why Preparing in Advance is Priceless: How MasterCard CEO Ajay Banga Planned Ahead for His New Leadership Role

Ajay Banga did a particularly good job at Master Card at embracing and leveraging his <u>Fuzzy Front End</u> (the time between the acceptance of the job and his start date). Many leaders fall into the trap of believing that leadership begins on day one of a new job, but Banga's actions are a good example of how leaders can use the time before then to <u>get a head start</u> in order to increase their chance of success.

Making the Move to MasterCard CEO

Ajay's transition from Citibank to MasterCard began even before the official announcement in June 2009 that he would join the company that summer. Arguably, his whole initial role as COO was one large Fuzzy Front End before he took over as CEO on July 1, 2010.

Ajay recently explained to me that this was all part of the three-stage plan created by his predecessor, Bob Selander, and the board: Stage 1) Ajay as COO reporting to Bob; Stage 2) Ajay as CEO with Bob still around; and Stage 3) Ajay as CEO with Bob not there.

Looking back on the transition, Ajay said Bob did a "*masterful*" job at allowing him to settle in and pick up pieces step-by-step without all the external and internal pressures getting dumped on him at the same time.

Throughout, Ajay leveraged his leadership skills in connecting with people. After 13 years at Citibank, he had an insider's view of the way things worked there. Ajay explained that it *"gets in your blood through a sort of reverse osmosis… But at MasterCard, I'm the outsider. So the only way I could get up to speed on the culture, what's working, what's not working, our competitive strengths and the like was to invest in listening"*.

Thus, he spent a lot of time doing just that. Ajay describes walking into offices at the headquarters, sitting down (or "flopping in a chair"[ii]) and saying *"I'm Ajay. Tell me about yourself."* or *"What can I do to help?"* or *"What should I not do"*. Good start, but not good enough. Then Ajay went out to meet *"people outside the big offices,"* traveling around the world to visit MasterCard's country offices to learn about their obstacles and strengths.

In general, Ajay chooses to be an optimist. In particular, he's convinced that the *"underlying secular growth is like a tailwind"* for MasterCard. As people around the world switch from cash to electronic payments, MasterCard is in the *"very rare"* position of being able to run before the wind. And if they can manage their business *"cleverly,"* they should gain share and grow in the low double digits. My guess is that they will.

Actions to Take Between Acceptance of a Job and the Start Date

This is a good example of the value of investing in relationships even before the start. There's no doubt that holding conversations with critical stakeholders before day one is a good thing. We used to think that was because the leader was more in control of his or her time before he or she had to deal with the day-to-day demands of the job. While that's still true, Brene Brown has helped me understand the Power of Vulnerability in connecting people. Asking for help before the start is such an act of vulnerability.

Other things people moving into new roles might consider doing during the Fuzzy Front End between acceptance and start include:

- **Identify key stakeholders:** up, across, down, both internally and externally, finding the people that control resources and can help you connect with others that control resources
- **Craft your message:** identify the platform for change, a vision of a brighter future, and a call to action; then putting those together into a master narrative that will drive your communication points throughout your start up

- Manage your **office setup**: make sure someone has put in place everything you need to do real work on day one. This probably includes things like a computer, phone, passwords, ID, office, assistant
- **Manage your personal/family setup**: situate yourself and family before you start so you can concentrate on work once you start.
- **Conduct pre-start meetings and phone calls**: connect with the most critical stakeholders. This has a huge impact.
- **Deploy an information gathering and learning plan**: get a half-step ahead of the curve. This is not so much about mastering anything as it is about learning enough to ask intelligent questions during your early days.
- **Plan your first 100-Days**:start with what you're going to do before day one, and include a specific plan for day one that reinforces your message, as well as the building blocks of accelerating your team over those first 100-days

This is a good example of step 3 of <u>The New Leader's Playbook</u>, **Embrace and Leverage the Fuzzy Front End Before Day One**

The time between acceptance and start is a gift you can use to rest and relax or to get a head start on your new role or next 100-days. Our experience has shown that those who use this fuzzy front end to put a plan in place, complete their pre-start preparation, and jump-start learning and relationships are far more likely to deliver better results faster than those who choose to rest and relax.

5,746 views Mar 1, 2011, 12:01pm

Walmart CEO Mike Duke Shifts Approach

Image by AFP/Getty Images via @daylife

Walmart's Mike Duke knows that we are all new leaders all the time. That's why organizational change management is an ongoing part of his life. Mike and his team are in touch with social, economic and political changes around the world; and they constantly monitor the results of their own choices and actions so they can adjust as needed. Q4 2010 is a case in point.

In touch with trends

Walmart continues to evolve its business in line with social trends like the growth of online shopping and consumers' search for healthier, affordable foods. As Mike put it in his Q4 earnings call:

"It's no surprise that we see growing opportunities in online shopping. I am pleased with the sales results of Walmart.com during the fourth quarter and expect e-commerce and multi-channel to play an increasingly important role across our business." and*

"We found there's a lot of interest in our global commitment to sustainable agriculture and our new initiative in the U.S. to make the food we sell healthier, and healthier foods more affordable for our customers. We were honored that First Lady Michelle Obama joined Bill Simon to launch this initiative last month."

The last quarter of 2010 highlights how fast things can change

While Walmart had a good year in 2010 overall, they got their merchandising mix wrong for the holidays in the U.S. Going into the holidays, they all felt good. As Mike said on November 16 – 39 days before Christmas:

"The U.S. team is taking the right steps to position our stores for the fourth quarter and for next year. I'm happy to see the response from our customers when I walk stores. They like our progress on merchandise. I might add, too, that just last week, when I visited stores here in the U.S. I loved the positive energy from our associates. Our associates are really excited about the changes in recent months. Also, I really like our holiday preparations."

But, as it turned out, they were not taking all the right steps. At the end of the quarter, Mike explained that Walmart's U.S. stores had a -1.8% comp store sales decline and that

"…many of the fourth quarter problems stem from merchandise assortment and presentation issues that contributed to customer traffic declines."

Walmart's US president, Bill Simon went further:

"We lost sales by having seasonal merchandise spread across too many areas of the store during the fourth quarter. Going forward, our seasonal merchandise for holidays such as Easter, Halloween and Christmas will have integrated targeted plans to present a more compelling presentation and product offering for our customers… Under the leadership of our new chief merchant, Duncan Mac Naughton, we will continue to work with our suppliers to deliver the broadest assortment possible at the lowest price in the market."

The point is not that Walmart got something wrong. We all get things wrong. The point is that they saw it, recognized it and adjusted with "a more compelling presentation" and a new chief merchant.

[Note 3 1/2 years later, Mike Duke's replacement, Doug McMillon ended up firing Bill Simon.]

Adjust to changing circumstances

One of the main advantages to adopting the mindset that we are all new leaders all the time is that you and your team will be ready at all times to adjust to changing circumstances and surprises. Remember, the ability to respond flexibly and fluidly is a hallmark of a high performing team.

Not all surprises are equal. Your first job is to sort them out to guide your own and your team's response. If it is a temporary, minor blip, keep your team focused on its existing priorities. If it is minor, but enduring, factor it into your ongoing evolution.

Major surprises are a different game. If they're temporary, you'll want to move into crisis or incident management. If they're enduring, you'll need to react and make some fundamental changes to deal with the new reality.

Part 4 of the 10-part series for new leaders

Stay tuned for the fourth post in my 10-part series on how new leaders and their teams can get done in 100 days what would normally take six to twelve months. The next column in *The New Leader's Playbook* series will highlight how Michael Brune, executive director of The Sierra Club, planned ahead for his first day on the job.

3,245 views Mar 2, 2011, 12:00pm

Powerful First Impressions: Michael Brune's Day One at The Sierra Club

Image by The Sierra Club via Flickr

Michael Brune took control of his first day as executive director of the Sierra Club last March. At least he took control of the things he could control. While he was not able to alter his 18-month-old son's sleep habits the night before so he could be well-rested, he did use available media to start communicating his message at work immediately – a critical component of transition management.

Owning Day One

As Brune explained to me in a phone interview, he took time out before he started to research the organization's history and think through what he wanted to get done on first day, first week, and first month.

"Since I knew I was going to go deep underwater, I wanted to have just a couple of big priorities that I wanted to stick to for at least the first month…Having those touchstones helped me to bring a little bit of order into the chaos of starting a new job."

Those touchstones included:

1. Being more solutions oriented. *"For years we'd been good at stopping (bad) things."* Now it seemed to be important to help move good things forward on *"symbolic and substantive ways"*.
2. *"Pull out what our bottom lines were"* - the things on which they could not compromise on as a way to provide a backstop beyond which we could not go.

3. Modernize the club, utilizing technology and polishing the brand to be more energetic, etc.

On his first day, Brune wrote in his blog:

"Today's my first day. I'm inspired and honored to be a part of such a

democratically-governed, volunteer-powered organization. From helping to protect Yosemite and millions of acres of wilderness to the more recent work of building powerful alliances with labor and impacted communities, Sierra Club volunteers and staff have played a pivotal role in many of the most important environmental victories over the past century.

But as effective as the organization has been over the past 118 years, we need to do our best work in the years ahead. The challenges -- and opportunities -- are too great." Read more: http://sierraclub.typepad.com/michaelbrune/page/4/#ixzz1DemeeDrv

Michael did several things right:

- He switched his identity and allegiance instantly, talking about himself as part of his new organization.
- He credited his predecessors and current team, telling people he hoped to follow their examples and build on their "victories."
- He started driving his message and communication points with what he said and what he did, wearing his own passion for the environment on his sleeve.
- He started by listening instead of *"talking, pontificating, declaring"*. His first morning he met with his executive team to get an update what they were doing and connect with work they'd already done. He learned where they thought the organization was strong and where they thought it needed help.
- Then, next, after listening to the executive team and taking that in, he had an all-staff, multi-office meeting to introduce himself to all and lay out his own initial observations about places needing attention

How to Plan Ahead for Day One

As you plan your own day one, here are a couple of things to keep in mind:

- *It is personal.* As a leader, you impact peoples' lives. Those people will try very hard to figure out you and your potential impact as soon as they can. They may even rush to judgment. Keep that in mind at all times.

- *Order counts.* Be circumspect about the order in which you meet with people and the timing of when you do what throughout Day One and your early days.

- *Messages matter.* Have a message. Know what you are going to say and not say. Have a bias toward listening. Know that strong opinions, long-winded introductions and efforts to prove yourself immediately are rarely, if ever good Day One tactics. People will be looking to form opinions early. Keep that in mind while deciding when to listen, when to share, what to ask, who to ask, and how you answer. When speaking keep it brief, on point and meaningful.

- *Location counts.* Think about where you will show up for work on Day One. Do not just show up at your designated office by default.

- *Signs and symbols count.* Be aware of all the ways in which you communicate, well beyond just words.

- *Timing counts.* Day One does not have to match the first day you get paid. Decide which day you want to communicate as Day One to facilitate other choices about order and location. (From The New Leader's 100-Day Action Plan)

This is a good example of step 4 of *The New Leader's Playbook*: **Take Control of Day One: Make a Powerful First Impression**

Everything is magnified on Day One, whether it's your first day in a new company, or the day of a big announcement. Everyone is looking for hints about what you think and what you're going to do. This is why it's so important to seed your message by paying particular attention to all the signs, symbols, and stories you deploy, and the order in which you deploy them. Make sure people are seeing and hearing things that will lead them to believe and feel what you want them to believe and feel about you and about themselves in relation to the future of the organization.

7,062 views Mar 9, 2011, 01:10pm

How the Red Cross's Charley Shimanski Inspires Others with Communication at the Heart of the Mission

Image via Wikipedia

Charley Shimanski's words inspire. His actions inspire. And they hold together because he firmly believes the importance of what he says and does. He exemplifies how new leaders can – and should – develop and implement communication efforts which inspire others to embrace and execute their missions. To put it simply: Be. Do. Say.

A few weeks ago, I had the opportunity to spend some time with Charley at his first Red Cross Disaster Response Directors conference. He recently moved from being CEO of the Red Cross's Denver chapter to heading up the organization's overall disaster response. This was his onboarding coming out party with his top 180 or so leaders. He knew that what he communicated and how he communicated it would be critical. But he wasn't worried about it.

The reason he wasn't worried was that the Red Cross's mission is core to his being. I asked Charley what was most important to him. He didn't hesitate:

"Our people. They are not only the most important asset we have, they are what makes the American Red Cross what it is. They represent that segment of society that is willing to roll up its sleeves to help someone that that they've never met before."

Charley went on to describe his thought process in preparing for the conference:

"I start by getting a sense of what I want them to feel when they're done hearing from me - what I want them to feel, not hear me say….I wanted them to feel that they are at the core of what we do, that our success is on their shoulders. I wanted them to feel proud."

He reinforced his sense of pride in the Red Cross on a continual basis throughout the conference, talking about how the organization is often *"the best part of someone's worst day,"* and punctuating others' success stories with *"How cool is that? You should feel that that's pretty cool. I hope you do."*

He also shared his own stories, describing how he first volunteered for disaster response 25 years ago when he saw a local TV news broadcast about a boy lost in the Colorado mountains and just showed up and helped.

Charley went on to discuss how he spent 25 years as a member of Colorado's Alpine Rescue Team and including a stint as President of the national Mountain Rescue Association – he mentioned how much the Red Cross has meant to him at very specific times in his life, particularly as a recipient of help from the Red Cross when he volunteered as a first-responder on rescues:

"There's no better cup of coffee than the cup of coffee served in a cardboard cup with a Red Cross on it because it's a cup of love."

Charley physically and emotionally puts his arms around people and draws them close to him, making them feel better about themselves. He does this face-to-face, one-on-one, and with his equally inspiring boss, Red Cross President and CEO Gail McGovern. Both of them reinforce the notion that disaster response is at *"the heart of the Red Cross's mission"*. He reinforces this message continually in large groups, interviews and through his Twitter account - warning people of risks, cajoling them to help and complimenting good work.

Charley tells the story of people in a restaurant who hear the sound of a significant car accident. As he describes it,

- Many will go to the window to see what happened.
- Some will go to the curb to see what happens next.
- But a small number of those patrons will rush to the accident scene to BE what happens next - helping out however they can to the best of their abilities.

Charley and the people he inspires through his communications are those who want to BE what happens next. Be. Do. Say.

Everything Communicates

Not surprisingly, since we live in the midst of a communication revolution, the guidelines for communicating are changing dramatically. As much as we would like to treat communication as a logical, sequential, ongoing communication campaign, in many cases, it's more essential to manage it as an iterative set of concurrent conversations:

1. Take into account the network of multiple stakeholders as you specifically identify your target audiences.
2. Discover and leverage your overarching message as the foundation for guiding iterative concurrent conversations by seeding and reinforcing communication points through a wide variety of media with no compromises on trustworthiness and authenticity.
3. Monitor and adjust as appropriate on an ongoing basis.

Don't hesitate to deploy an old school logical, sequential communication campaign when appropriate – though we expect that to be the case less and less over time.

This is a good example of step 5 of _The New Leader's Playbook_: **Drive Action by Activating and Directing an Ongoing Communication Network (Including Social Media)**

Where the emphasis used to be on logical, sequential, targeted, ongoing communication campaigns, the communication revolution has made it essential to manage multiple, concurrent, ever-evolving conversations across an ever-changing network of stakeholders. Leverage your core message as the foundation for those conversations by seeding and reinforcing communication points through a wide variety of media with no compromises on trustworthiness and authenticity.

7,619 views Mar 16, 2011, 11:57am

How CEO Sam Martin is Driving the Imperative to Overhaul A&P

Supermarket giant A&P was in dire need of a major financial and operational overhaul. Its problems had been mounting for a while. It was clear to Sam Martin when he took over as CEO in July of 2010 that he was going to have to apply the frameworks and leadership skills he had developed over his career to lead the organization through a substantial turnaround covering every aspect of the business.

According to Sam five things are always necessary for a turnaround:

1. Installing a strong management team
2. Strengthening liquidity
3. Reducing structural and operating costs
4. Improving the value proposition for customers
5. Enhancing customers' in-store experience

Since each situation is unique, the challenge is figuring out which of those five are in place and which need to be addressed. At A&P, Sam faced a situation in which "*all five were woefully in need of being addressed.*" He was concerned that the situation would deteriorate and that he needed a "path to success" so he could rally the larger team behind his view to success – fast. As Sam explained to me when I interviewed him,

"It was essential to have an articulated plan available to share robustly around the organization and with all our stakeholders…If (our employees) are not properly armed with the right information, they will give the wrong message – because they're going to give a message anyway. So getting the right message in the right hands quickly is important and essential to getting off on the right foot and having any chance of success in the outcome."

In particular, Sam reviewed what had made A&P a great company across vast distances:

1. Innovative spirit
2. Development of the core people including management
3. Focus on the customer

He then mapped out the imperative and went to work, implementing the various aspects of the plan:

- Announcing the closing of 25 stores to "strengthen A&P's operating foundation" (August 13)
- Hiring Paul Hertz as EVP of operations (August 18)
- Hiring Carter Knox as head of HR (August 19)
- Installing Jake Brace as Chief Administrative Officer because of his "successful turnaround experience" (August 21)
- Appointing Tom O'Boyle to head merchandising, marketing, and supply and logistics, completing the team to lead the "turnaround initiative"

By the October 22 earnings call* Martin was able to say with confidence that *"there should be no doubt that this management team is moving with urgency."*

Leading an organization into and through Chapter 11 or any turnaround is tough stuff. People generally don't like change and they certainly don't like uncertain change. Any time an organization goes through this, there are tremendous unknowns and stress. While it's in no way certain that Martin and his team will be able to help A&P regain its former glory across all of its previous vast distances, they have been clear and consistent in driving the turn-around imperative. That helps a lot.

The burning imperative is a cornerstone building block and involves creating an understanding among team members what they are supposed to do immediately and how this works with the larger aspirations of the team and the organization. Everything pivots off a business' mission, vision, objectives, goals, strategies, plans and values. So think through these components:

Headline: The all-encapsulating phrase or tagline that defines your burning imperative

Mission: Why are we here, why does the business exist, what business are we in?

Vision: Future picture — what do we want to become; where are we going?

Values: Beliefs and moral principles that guide attitudes, decisions, and actions

Objectives: Broadly defined, qualitative performance requirements

Goals: The quantitative measures of the objectives that define success

Strategies: Broad choices around how the team will achieve its objectives

Plans: The most important projects and initiatives that will bring each strategy to fruition.

What Sam Martin has done at A&P is a good example of step 6: **Embed a Strong Burning Imperative**

The burning imperative is a sharply defined, intensely shared, and purposefully urgent understanding from each of the team members of what they are "supposed to do, now." Get this created and bought into early on—even if it's only 90 percent right. You, and the team, will adjust and improve along the way.

2,019 views Mar 23, 2011, 12:00pm

Royal Caribbean's CEO Exemplifies How to Leverage Milestones

Tracking milestones is not a revolutionary business idea. However, the idea of using them as a team-building tool is new to most leaders and their teams. Royal Caribbean's CEO, Richard Fain, fully appreciates the power of milestones and exemplifies how other leaders can utilize them to keep projects on track and recognize employee achievements.

Milestones for Project Management

Richard's emphasis on milestones is not a surprise, as ship builders have been leveraging milestones' emotional impact for millennia. Ship builders celebrate "keel laying" as the formal start of construction, naming, stepping the mast (accompanied by placing coins under the mast for good luck), christening (accompanied by breaking a bottle of champagne over the bow), a whole range of trials, "sail away", hand over, and my personal favorite - onboarding the new captain.

As Richard explained to me,

"If you don't establish early on key milestones - long-term milestones rather than the short-term milestones - you get caught in the 'next week' syndrome. I can't think of a project that we are doing or have done (during which we do not) get to a key point and everybody says 'We're going to know so much more next week or the week after.' And so the focus shifts to next week or the week after and we all desperately wait for that period. Meanwhile the longer-term milestone goes by the wayside.

So what we tend to do is say we need to know where we're going. We need to know what we expect to have at the end. And so we talk a lot about our end point rather than the waypoints."

Milestones for Team Building

What Richard does particularly well is leverage milestones both as a way to keep big projects on track – like building a ship, a new computer system, or a major marketing program – and to keep smaller projects on track. They also provide him with excuses to encourage all involved along the way. He goes to major events. He participates in new ship trials so he can experience the excitement of how the ship performs. Then he shares that excitement with others in his meetings, talks, videos, blog, and all forms of communication.

Richard talked about how "<u>letting people know you care is of surpassing value</u>" in an interview with Knowledge@Wharton. The links with his approach to milestones come through. He's built a team of people that try to surpass – and he gives them milestones to beat. He knows that people value recognition – and he leverages milestone ceremonies to recognize their achievements whether it's the first time people can actually walk on board and see a ship, or the first look at the prototype of a new computer system.

Royal Caribbean likes to build models so people can see and touch tangible things and know what they are going to do. They model staterooms, software, and marketing materials. When a project gets to a certain point, they give it a name. *"It's interesting how giving that project a name galvanizes people around it – because it makes it more tangible to them."*

One of its big projects was the creation of a central gathering area on the ship "Oasis of the Seas." This area – which is aptly named Central Park -- is located in the middle of the ship and opens to the sky for five decks. To celebrate the design, it created a full-size model of part of this open space in the massive hangar-like building where parts of the ship were being built in Finland.   Also, the company treated the whole team to an alfresco fine dining experience so they could celebrate the space.

"It was a magical evening …We were having a lovely cruise dinner in Finland (in early Spring – when it's still cold outside)… It made us all realize how special the space would be and that it was worthy of the effort to really make sure that not only was the overall space good, but that all the details were perfect."

Once they know you care, then you can challenge them. As Fain said in a recent interview with Adam Bryant for the New York Times, *"My experience is that people love to be challenged. If the challenge is reasonable, or even slightly unreasonable, they love it and they rise to the occasion. There's just no question. People love to be challenged and they love to show off their skills and talents."* Aggressive, but doable milestones create just such a challenge.

Establish a Process to Track Milestones

Compiling milestones is a waste of time if you do not have an efficient, effective and clear process in place to track them – and avoid the "next week" syndrome.

Define them and begin tracking and managing to them immediately. Use the process to establish and reinforce expected team norms.

1. Get milestones in place.
2. Track them and manage them as a team on a frequent and regular basis.
3. Implement a milestone management process with a particular emphasis on solving problems and celebrating wins – as a team. (With your own version of a lovely al fresco cruise dinner in a warehouse.)

This is a good example of step 7 of *The New Leader's Playbook*: **Exploit Key Milestones to Drive Team Performance**

The milestone tool is straightforward and focuses on mapping and tracking and what is getting done by when by whom. High-performing team leaders take that basic tool to a whole new level, exploiting it to inspire and enable people to work together as a team!

2,240 views Mar 30, 2011, 11:26am

IBM's Sue Hed Shows How Early Wins Get You Ahed of the Curve

When Sue Hed returned from Europe to lead IBM's alliance with Oracle, she knew she was dealing with a classic case of co-opetition. IBM and Oracle were competing and cooperating at the same time. As Sue explained to me on a plane ride over the sound of screaming children, the thing that brought all the players together was a *"need to work together to create value for the end client."*

Both her team and her counterparts at Oracle were particularly interested in pursuing growth in the middle-markets. Her idea was to go after this with a three-pronged approach:

1 Target Top 5 Prospects and Channel Partners

The first prong was to target the top 5 prospects and channel partners in each market for IBM and Oracle. These people were going to require face-to-face presence to win them over and service their business.

2 Leverage Social Media with Other Channel Partners

The second prong was a way to go after the 80% of the rest of the channel partners that were going to account for 20% of the business. While each one of them was relatively small, there was a long tail. Her approach there was to leverage social media like LinkedIn and Twitter to build awareness.

3 Deploy Telemarketing to Get Feedback

The third prong was to deploy telemarketing as get feedback from all the customers and prospects on how to drive into the channel. While it wasn't going to be cost-effective to have face-to-face meetings with the smaller customers, Sue and her team needed to keep their ears to the ground one way or another. Telemarketing allowed them to have those conversations.

Sue's milestones were relatively straightforward:

1. Define the scope of the IBM-Oracle partnership. Build the database.
2. Assess the market and figure out how they could best create value together.
3. Get the buy in of the sales organizations to their approach.
4. Validate the approach
5. Roll it out

Early Wins

The early wins came into play as a way of validating the approach. Sue chose to pilot the programs in Australia and Turkey. Her logic was to *"validate and test by starting small, picking a more manageable geography or two before going into bigger markets like the UK or the USA"*.

Sue over-invested in those first pilots going out into the field herself to work with the teams to make the contacts, establish the relationships, close the deals, and over-see the implementation of the programs. It worked locally and gave the team a head start elsewhere. As Sue describes it:

"The buy-in has been great in other countries because they saw the success and had testimonials from their peers."

That sports fans is exactly why it makes so much sense to over-invest in early wins.

Our early win prescription is relatively simple:

1. **Select one or two early wins from your milestones list:**

   - Choose early wins that will make a meaningful external impact.

   - Select early wins that your boss will want to talk about.

   - Pick early wins that you are sure you can deliver.

   - Choose early wins that will model important behaviors.

   - Pick early wins that would not have happened if you had not been there.

2. **Establish early wins in your second month and deliver by your sixth month:**

   - Early means early. Make sure you select early wins in your first 60 days that you and the team can deliver by the end of your sixth month. Select them early. Communicate them early. Deliver them early.

   - Make sure the team understands the early wins and has bought in to delivering them on time.

   - This will give your bosses the concrete results they need when someone asks how you are doing.

3. **Over-invest resources toward early wins to over-deliver:**

   - Do not skimp on your early wins. Allocate resources in a manner that will ensure timely delivery. Put more resources than you think you should need against these early opportunities so your team is certain to deliver them better and faster than anyone thought was possible.

   - Stay alert. Adjust quickly. As the leader, stay close and stay involved on the progress of your early wins and react immediately if they start to fall even slightly off track or behind schedule.

4. **Celebrate and Communicate Early Wins:**

- As your first early wins are achieved, celebrate the accomplishment with the entire team. This is important and should not be overlooked.

- In conjunction with your communication campaign, make sure your early wins are communicated as appropriate.

What Sue did is a good example of step 8 of The New Leader's Playbook, **Over-invest in Early Wins to Build Team Confidence**

Early wins are all about credibility and confidence. People have more faith in people who have delivered. You want your boss to have confidence in you. You want team members to have confidence in you, in themselves, and in the plan for change that has emerged. Early wins fuel that confidence.

826 views Mar 31, 2011, 11:26am

Will Robert Gibbs Find a Friend in Facebook?

Image by Getty Images via @daylife

A Tool to Help Gibbs (or Anyone Else) Assess Cultural Fit

Young, hip, innovative, fresh, forward thinking; all adjectives you would use to describe Facebook. The same words don't immediately come to mind for Robert Gibbs, who is old enough to be the CEO's father and has just departed one of the most closed-off, buttoned-up work sites in the country – The White House.

This situation, although magnified in this instance given the high-profile nature of Facebook and Gibbs, is common in Corporate America where similar cultural transitions happen all the time as part of executive onboarding. To help Gibbs, Mark Zuckerberg and everyone else moving through the motions of this frequent occurrence of transition management, we have developed a tool which will be featured in the upcoming edition of The New Leader's 100-Day Action Plan that can assist in figuring out if the fit is right.

FIT

The issue is that "fit" is hard to define, hard to figure out in advance, a critical predictor of success, and the number one stated reason for failure. (Though, of course, the stated reason for failure doesn't often match the actual reason for failure.)

Worse, an organization's culture itself is hard to define and rarely actually matches the stated or self-described culture. For example, what famous company's cultural values included "Communication, Respect, Integrity and Excellence"?.......... ENRON. Making it clear that not everyone does what they say they should do.

To evaluate culture effectively we believe in utilizing a BRAVE framework: Behaviors, Relationships, Attitudes, Values, and Environment. We further propose that matching what an individual has become comfortable with and what's really going on in an organization can give you a read on cultural fit.

-

BRAVE Character and Culture

Behave: How people act, make decisions, control the business, etc.

Relate: How people communicate with others (including mode, manner and frequency), engage in intellectual debate, manage conflict, assign credit and blame[1], etc.

Attitude: How people feel about the organization's purpose, mission, vision, identify with the subgroup, group, organization as a whole, basis for power, etc.

Values: The underlying assumptions beliefs, intentions, approach to learning, risk, time horizons, etc.

Environment: The work environment in terms of office space protocols, décor, etc.

-

The big potential disconnects between Gibbs and Facebook are in the areas of Relationships and Environment. On the one hand, it's as hard to imagine a more walled, formal office setting than the White House and a more informal office setting than the open cacophony of Facebook's hip geek gongers. On the other hand, I suspect Gibbs could adjust to that.

The real issues are likely going to be in the way the two groups relate. Gibbs has gotten used to very high-level, very formal communication.

Facebookers are formal in their programming and proudly anti-formal in their personal interactions. Even more telling, while Facebookers have been spending their time dealing with new tools for people to connect with each other at a surface level, Gibbs has been involved in in-depth intellectual debates about some of the world's most fundamental, intractable problems.

I'm not sure how Gibbs and Zuckerberg and his tribe will fit together. What's scary is neither are they and neither are most people looking to onboard into new organizations. Hopefully this tool can help. Click here to get a paper emailed to you on using the tool to assess cultural fit.

This is one part of step 1 of _The New Leader's Playbook_: **Position Yourself for Success**

There are several components of this including positioning yourself for a leadership role, selling before you buy, mapping and avoiding the most common land mines, uncovering hidden risks in the organization, role, and fit, and choosing the right approach for your transition type.

3,040 views Apr 6, 2011, 11:33am

Chiquita CEO Fernando Aguirre on Inspiring and Enabling Others

When the more experienced speakers at CEO Connection's CEO Boot Camps are asked to look back on their executive training and careers and reflect on what they most regret, every single one of them has talked about not moving faster on people. As Chiquita CEO Fernando Aguirre told me in a recent interview:

I'm a big believer that you need to move very quickly and adapt to the changing circumstances in the marketplace.

So, when Chiquita's business in Europe ran into "significant headwinds" last year along with the rest of the industry, Fernando was indeed ready to move very quickly.

Brian Kocher had dealt with very similar challenges here (in North America) *in the last three years or so and he did very well. He had accomplished significant goals and he had more than delivered on his objectives. And* (moving him to Europe) *gave me an opportunity to give him experience outside of North America…always a good thing for an executive on the rise.*

While Fernando does not hesitate to make such moves when he needs to, his first choice approach is to develop and encourage his people so they can deal with the headwinds they face where they are. For him, *"It's all about personal goals."* He goes out of his way to let people know that,

I want to help you develop yourselves as leaders.

I want to help you develop yourselves as professionals.

But I also care very much about your personal side.

For example, Fernando met Leo Urzua during his stint on CBS's
<u>Undercover Boss</u>. Leo was the harvest coordinator who tried to teach
Fernando how to pick and prune lettuce. Tried. Failed. However, in
meeting Leo and getting to know him, Fernando was inspired by Leo's
quest to become a U.S. citizen, in a way seeing a version of himself and his
own journey from immigrant to CEO. Fernando committed to helping
Leo. Succeeded. Leo was recently sworn in as a citizen in Yuma
Arizona. The keynote speaker at that ceremony? ....Fernando Aguirre.

While you, as a leader, will certainly do this in your own inimitable way,
you must Acquire, Develop, Encourage, Plan, and Transition talent over
time.

Let your mission inform the ideal organization and help you identify the
required roles.

Let your vision then help you identify which of the required roles must be
best in class.

Then match performance, strengths, motivation and fit of individuals and
roles:

- Support and develop high performers in right roles. (Feed them
  more than just bananas.)

- Improve performance of low performers in right roles. (Invest here.)

- Evolve high performers in wrong role to better roles over time. (The trickiest challenge of all.)

- Move low performers in wrong role to better role now.

Some of your most painful choices are going to be in this area; trying to please everybody will lead to pleasing nobody. Choosing to act on people who are in the wrong roles now or will soon be in the wrong roles is generally not the most enjoyable part of leadership. But it is an essential part.

Remember that you can't separate the business element from the human element. This is golden rule time. While not all of us will travel from immigrant to CEO, we're all on a journey. Treat others with the dignity and respect with which you would want them to treat you on your journey. When it's their turn, they will.

Fernado's efforts are a good example of step 9 of _The New Leader's Playbook_: **Secure ADEPT People in the Right Roles and Deal with Inevitable Resistance**

Make your organization ever more ADEPT by Acquiring, Developing, Encouraging, Planning, and Transitioning talent:

- **Acquire**: Recruit, attract, and onboard the right people
- **Develop**: Assess and build skills and knowledge
- **Encourage**: Direct, support, recognize, and reward
- **Plan**: Monitor, assess, plan career moves over time
- **Transition**: Migrate to different roles as appropriate

1,997 views Apr 13, 2011, 10:38am

QlikTech CEO Galvanizes Team, Delivers 50% Growth

QlikTech's CEO Lars Bjork knows that sustaining extraordinary growth requires rejuvenating the team on a regular basis. That's why each year for the last 12 years every single one of his employees, from senior executives to the cleaning staff, has participated in a five-day session that celebrates employees and connects the company's global workforce while building their leadership skills. He's absolutely convinced that this is one critical element to their having been able to sustain a 50% Compound Annual Growth Rate for five years.

QlikTech's annual "revaccination" is an opportunity for Lars to reiterate the corporate message and for employees to engage face-to-face with their colleagues from around the world. In homage to QlikTech's Swedish roots, the same rock band is flown in from Sweden every year (7 years in a row so far). But more importantly, They spend a full day on "value activities," honoring people that have lived the company's core values: Challenge, Move fast, Open and straightforward, Teamwork for results, Take responsibility.

For example, this past year, one mid-level HR person had been given responsibility for a new territory.

"In a few months she established processes and put into place methods of how to hire a lot of people in a short time that I think surprised the rest of us. She was given that responsibility and she took it."

The full organization gets a chance to nominate people for these honors. After a series of reviews, the top five are recognized each year at the closing dinner.

Teamwork for results

Lars is a big believer that "Your only job as a leader and a manager is to make sure your team is successful." He suggests that "If you want to grow at a high pace, hire the best and get out of the way because you are the bottleneck. If everything is going to go through you, every single small decision, nothing is going to happen because you only have 24 hours."

Lars has *"A consensus driven leadership style. It's all about motivating people, empowering them, involving them in decision making. And out of that you will get more engaged, more loyal and clearly more motivated people because the feel they contribute to something."*

Better Results Over Time

An organization or team's performance is based on aligning its people, plans, and practices around a shared purpose. This involves getting the right *people* in the right roles with the right support, getting clarity around the strategies and action steps included in *plans,* and getting *practices* in place that enable people to work together in a systematic and effective way. The heart of this is the organization's *purpose.* For that to be genuinely shared, it must be meaningful, clearly understood and rewarding for each of the people contributing to make its aspiration real.

Look at what Lars is doing. His passion for getting the right people in the right roles in sync with the organization's culture oozes out of his every pore. He's crystal clear on his strategic choices and plans. He's evolving, reinforcing and celebrating good practices at every step. And he pulls everyone together once a year, along with smaller groups on an ongoing basis to reinforce their purpose of simplifying decision making for business users across organizations.

What QlikTech is doing is a good example of step 10 of *The New Leader's Playbook*: **Evolve People, Plans, and Practices to Capitalize on Changing Circumstances**

By the end of your first 100-Days, you should have made significant steps toward aligning your people, plans, and practices around a shared purpose. Remember, this is not a one-time event but, instead, something that will require constant, ongoing management and Darwinian improvement.

1,082 views Apr 20, 2011, 11:38am

Cusack Capital CEO's Second Act Disaster (Onboarding Done Wrong)

Image via Wikipedia

Much discussed Greenwich hedge fund LeeWell Capital was cranking out strong, steady returns in April 2008 when James Cusack joined as head of sales. Cusack was hired to ramp up growth and grab market share while the competition stumbled. He had been CEO of Cusack Capital, a significantly smaller hedge fund that closed at the end of 2007. Working for the legendary Cy Leeser at LeeWell Capital seemed like a strong second act, an opportunity to make big money and regain industry stature.

Some leaders manage <u>executive onboarding</u> extremely well, but James Cusack did almost everything wrong. I interviewed Cusack about his second act disaster and he shared the following.

"I was incredibly relieved to find a big upside job in financial services when the capital markets were in such turmoil. In retrospect, my decision to join LeeWell Capital was driven by emotion, not sound career management. After my hedge fund failed, I was deeply in debt and, honestly, feeling pretty desperate."

Cusack's first mistake was his failure to move from "seller" to "buyer" after the job offer. He conducted virtually no due diligence before accepting. James Googled Cy Leeser, read trade periodicals, and talked to friends in the hedge fund industry who worked in Greenwich, Connecticut near LeeWell Capital.

"But that was it. I had no opportunity to work my way around the inside of LeeWell because the offer came so quickly. "

Due diligence is about understanding and mitigating risk. At a minimum Cusack should have thought like a buyer and insisted on a few days to look long and hard at three of the seven potential **onboarding landmines** : *organizational risks*, *role risks*, and *personal risks*. If he had, he would have turned down the job and avoided an extremely painful experience. If Cusack had met with the head trader and reviewed even the most cursory internal documents, he would have questioned the viability of LeeWell Capital's claimed competitive advantage ("the secret sauce"). Lack of sustainable competitive advantage is the biggest organizational risk I can think of.

Cusack's second mistake was his failure to use the valuable time between accepting and starting to prepare his 100-Day Action Plan and have pre-boarding conversations with key stakeholders.

"After I said yes, I breathed a sigh of relief! I spent five days with my wife. Took a break. Tried to sort out my personal financial problems. It was the calm between the storms. I did everything but look at the job."

James could not afford to waste a moment of prep time. After all, he was an investment professional moving into a sales and marketing role. He would have to simultaneously perform and learn a whole new skill set. And failure was not an option. If anyone needed to use the time between acceptance and start to do onboarding prep, it was James Cusack.

I asked James this question during our recent interview, "Why you? Why did Cy Leeser hire you, of all people?" James' answer:

"At the time it didn't make any sense, why me. But Cy and I clicked. The rapport felt good. My strength was knowledge of the markets and investing acumen, not business development. But I thought I could do anything. I was naive. I did not even consider why Cy wanted me. And, of course, it turned out he didn't really want me, he wanted my personal connections."

There is much more to this story of a second act disaster – onboarding gone wrong. The first 100 Days? Well, they spun out of control. The good news is James Cusack doesn't actually exist. He's a character in The Gods of Greenwich, a new novel by Norb Vonnegut. Hopefully, if Norb gives future characters new leadership roles, he will inspire and enable them to do a better job with their own onboarding or the onboarding of people they bring in to work with them.

2,669,072 views Apr 27, 2011, 11:45am

Top Executive Recruiters Agree There Are Only Three True Job Interview Questions

The only three true job interview questions are:

1.   Can you do the job?
2.   Will you love the job?
3.   Can we tolerate working with you?

That's it. Those three. Think back, every question you've ever posed to others or had asked of you in a job interview is a subset of a deeper in-depth follow-up to one of these three key questions. Each question may be asked using different words, but every question, however it is phrased, is just a variation on one of these topics: Strengths, Motivation, and Fit.

Click here for more on How to Become the 'Must Hire' Candidate in a Job Interview

Can You Do the Job? - Strengths

Executive Search firm Heidrick & Struggles CEO, Kevin Kelly explained to me that it's not just about the technical skills, but also about leadership and interpersonal strengths. Technical skills help you climb the ladder. As you get there, managing up, down, and across become more important.

You can't tell by looking at a piece of paper what some of the strengths and weaknesses really are…We ask for specific examples of not only what's been successful but what they've done that hasn't gone well or a task they've, quite frankly, failed at and how they learned from that experience and what they'd do different in a new scenario.

Not only is it important to look at the technical skill set they have…but also the strengths on what I call the EQ side of the equation in terms of getting along and dealing or interacting with people.

Will You Love the Job? -Motivation

Cornerstone International Group CEO, Bill Guy emphasizes the changing nature of motivation,

…younger employees do not wish to get paid merely for working hard—just the reverse: they will work hard because they enjoy their environment and the challenges associated with their work…. Executives who embrace this new management style are attracting and retaining better employees.

Can We Tolerate Working With You? - Fit

Continuing on with our conversation, Heidrick's Kelly went on to explain the importance of cultural fit:

A lot of it is cultural fit and whether they are going to fit well into the organization… The perception is that when (senior leaders) come into the firm, a totally new environment, they know everything. And they could do little things such as send emails in a voicemail culture that tend to negatively snowball over time. Feedback or onboarding is critical. If you don't get that feedback, you will get turnover later on.

He made the same point earlier in an interview with Smart Business, referencing Heidrick's internal study of 20,000 searches.

40 percent of senior executives leave organizations or are fired or pushed out within 18 months. It's not because they're dumb; it's because a lot of times culturally they may not fit in with the organization or it's not clearly articulated to them as they joined.

Preparing for Interview

If you're the one doing the interviewing, get clear on what strengths, motivational and fit insights you're looking for before you go into your interviews.

If you're the one being interviewed, prepare by thinking through examples that illustrate your **strengths**, what **motivates** you about the organization and role you're interviewing for, and the **fit** between your own preferences and the organization's Behaviors, Relationships, Attitudes, Values, and

Environment (BRAVE). But remember that interviews are exercises in solution selling. They are not about you.

Think of the interview process as a chance for you to show your ability to solve the organization and interviewer's problem. That's why you need to highlight strengths in the areas most important to the interviewers, talk about how you would be motivated by the role's challenges, and discuss why you would be a BRAVE fit with the organization's culture.

Executive Onboarding

Once you've got the job, be sure to pay attention to <u>executive onboarding</u>, the key to accelerating success and reducing risk in a new job.

6,033 views May 4, 2011, 11:35am

Why Apple is Doing Well Without Steve Jobs

Image by Getty Images via @daylife

In January 2011 Apple CEO Steve Jobs announced he was taking a medical leave of absence. Apple COO, Tim Cook, is now responsible for the company's day-to-day operations.

So far so good. I'd like to call attention to some of the leadership skills Cook is evidencing and things he's doing particularly well as the interim head of the company:

1. Keep the interim in interim

2. Focus on the task

3. Eschew the perks

Keep the interim in interim

There are different sorts of interim assignments. These include:

- Holding the fort until we find the right person, which absolutely will not be you.
- On probation with a good chance of becoming permanent.
- Doing the job as a developmental opportunity on the way to something else.

Cook and Apple are not talking about any of these. It's not clear how long his interim assignment will last, whether there will another interim assignment after that, or if it will become permanent. Cook is acting and talking like he is filling Jobs' shoes until Jobs comes back.

There is every reason to believe that first prize for Cook, and all involved, is for Jobs to come back. In Cook's commencement address to Auburn's graduating class he said, *"I am where I am in life because of (my parents, teachers)…and Steve Jobs. "He also went on to explain that "five minutes into my initial interview with Steve, I wanted to throw caution and logic to the wind and join Apple."* Cook knows his own strengths and recognizes Jobs' "creative genius." He's acting like it's an interim role because he truly, sincerely hopes it's an interim role.

Focus on the task

Cook is staying focused on the task at hand. He revealed one of his core mantra's in the Auburn talk:

In business as in sports, the vast majority of victories are determined before the beginning of the game. We rarely control the timing of opportunities, but we can control our preparation… Make sure your execution lives up to your preparation.

As far as Cook and Jobs' team are concerned, Apple is continuing its turnaround. There is no way they are going to falter on execution – if they have anything to say about it. Cook has been Jobs' number two and part of the inner management circle for long enough to step up and work with the rest of the team to keep things running as they should, and as Jobs would expect.

Eschew the perks

Cook is carrying the title of COO, not Interim CEO. The most effective interim executives don't take the fancier title, don't take over the fancier office and simply don't do anything fancy. They engage fully with the work itself while eschewing the perks of the job – basically, focusing their efforts on the least prestigious, highest impact tasks and leaving the glory to others.

Cook is doing this well. If needed, he gives the presentations – his way, not Jobs' way. When possible, he yields the stage to Jobs. Witness the ipad 2 announcement and Jobs' comments on location tracking.

It isn't tough to understand why this works. People appreciate a leader that inspires and enables others. People do not appreciate a leader that engages in self-inspiration and self-enablement. Apple is doing well without Jobs because Cook is doing things the way Jobs wants them done, not necessarily the way Jobs would do them himself.

This is a good example of step 1 of _The New Leader's Playbook_: **Position Yourself for Success**

There are several components of this including positioning yourself for a leadership role, selling before you buy, mapping and avoiding the most common land mines, uncovering hidden risks in the organization, role, and fit, and choosing the right approach for your transition type. (Including an interim role.)

5,082 views May 11, 2011, 11:30am

Follow Three Imperatives in Starting a Successful Service Business

Image by boellstiftung via Flickr

Robert Rigby-Hall and Glenn Kaufman are not onboarding into new leadership roles. They are creating them as they start up the HR LeaderCamp, a leadership program for high-potential Human Resource talent.

On the one hand, both Robert and Glenn are seasoned business executives who have led organizations in the past. On the other hand, this is their first start up, so they are paying particular attention to following the three imperatives for starting a successful service business, including:

1. Be different

2. Be strong

3. Be committed

Be Different

Robert and Glenn think they have a differentiated idea. They expect to run three-day camps for high-potential HR leaders to sharpen their leadership skills. This will be achieved with the help of seasoned, industry-recognized Human Resource executives, along with guest speakers who are creating trends adopted by global corporations.

As Glenn explained to me, "HR *are the shoemaker's kids. We are always creating programs to develop the company's leaders, but not ourselves. We started HR LeaderCamp to address this gap in a pragmatic, non-academic way.*"

The critical question is whether or not this is really different from the other training opportunities available. If it is, they'll have a chance at success. If it's not, they'll end up competing on price – not a good way to make money over any period of time in a service business.

Be Strong

One of the concepts they are sure to teach their campers is that teams always beat individuals. Robert and Glenn are starting this together. As a team of two, they are already ahead of any individual. But they realize they will need to supplement their expertise with other cutting-edge HR experts to deliver the kind of high-value programs they envision.

Also, they are connecting with other experts to help with their start-up, an "extended family" that are providing insight into marketing, social media and logistics. If, as Drucker suggests, "The purpose of business is to create and keep a customer," Robert and Glenn can create the innovative programs that will keep customers, but will need help finding them.

They recognize this. Robert's perspective is that "*By focusing on a narrow niche - practical business skills for HR taught by seasoned leaders - we're using all our friends, business networks and reputation. It's gratifying to see so many people believe in us and want to be a part of it.*"

Be Committed

As anyone that's ever done it will tell you, starting up a service business is hard work. Don't even start if you're not committed to business development, client satisfaction and continual improvement. You won't be successful.

Business Development

It's not enough to do great work. You have to convince others to pay you for doing it. Do not underestimate how difficult and time-consuming this is going to be over time. If you don't love selling and aren't good at it, consider a different route.

Glenn gets this: "*We are trying to position our services as part of the HR value chain. If HR talent is thinking like the business clients that they serve, then everybody gains. HR LeaderCamp is all about getting HR close to their internal customers, the business leaders. This is why we're getting daily feedback from CHRO's and potential customers to understand and incorporate their needs into HR LeaderCamp's design.*"

Client Satisfaction

Very quickly, the best source of new business will be from existing clients. As Tony Hseigh's Zappos exemplifies, over-delivering at every step is the single best way to build advocates and fans. Make sure you're over-delivering on the most important components of your strategy, which is to the centerpiece of how you are different from your competitors.

Robert is passionate about this: "*We both have very aligned values and care about going that extra mile for our customers, so we'll be measuring satisfaction and we'll refine the program so we're always exceeding expectations!*"

Continual Improvement

If you're not evolving, you're stagnating. And if you're stagnating, someone else is going to catch up and pass you by. So ceaselessly improve your strategic focus, tactical capacity and executional excellence. This is why Robert and Glenn have already started working on their next levels of service and new programs that complement the niche they are developing.

This is a good example of step 1 of *The New Leader's Playbook*: **Position Yourself for Success**

There are several components of this including positioning yourself for a leadership role, selling before you buy, mapping and avoiding the most common land mines, uncovering hidden risks in the organization, role, and fit, and choosing the right approach for your transition type.

648 views May 18, 2011, 11:40am

The Secret to Jets Coach Rex Ryan Winning Record is His "Whole Team" Approach

Image by Getty Images via @daylife

It's hard to balance the leadership skills, strengths and needs of individual performers with those of the team as a whole. It's also hard for some individuals to concentrate on what they need to do without getting distracted by what's going on around them. New York Jets National Football League Coach Rex Ryan thinks these are false tradeoffs. As he told NPR's Steve Inskeep,

My dad taught me early in my coaching career that football is an easy game, made complicated by coaches. And so what we do ... with our defense, we'll actually have the entire defense in a meeting and we'll teach the entire defense to everybody. Everybody is in the same room, and there's accountability because you all know each other's jobs. You teach the whole defense to everybody and it may sound complicated [but] it's not.

Jets player Jason Taylor has seen the value in this approach for a long time. As he told ESPN's Jane McManus,

In some defenses you can learn your job, and as long as you know your job you can kind of get lost with what everybody else needs to do....I've always been a guy that I want to understand the whole defense.

It's not that Ryan is asking individuals to subordinate their hopes and needs to the team. He's asking them to leverage those hopes and needs to make the team do better. Jets player Jim Leonhard explained it this way to *The New York Times' Toni Monkovic,*

This system puts guys in positions to make big plays. This coaching staff does a great job of determining what each player's strengths are and trying to put them in positions to utilize those strengths on a play-to-play basis, not just game-to-game; play-to-play, throughout every game. As a player, you have to love that. You have to love knowing that going into every game you feel like you have the opportunity to be that guy that makes the difference.

Teams Are Made Up of Individuals

You can learn a lot about a manager by the debris he or she leaves in his or her wake. Some managers leave a trail of broken and disillusioned people behind them who never recover from getting run over by the manager. Other managers leave behind high-performing leaders that go on to do great things. Click here for more on wake management.

High-performing leaders must be part of a high-performing team while leading at the same time. They must be able to take advantage of *"the opportunity to be that guy that makes the difference,"* <u>and</u> they must be able to create the opportunity for someone else to be that guy. A big part of this is everyone knowing how the whole team works so individuals know when to pass and when to take the shot. It's important for people to understand team dynamics <u>and</u> what motivates the other individuals on the team.

Organizations Are Made Up of Sub-Groups

Every large organization has sub-groups. Some sub-groups work well together. Some behave like silos. Just as Ryan puts his defensive linemen, linebackers and backs in the same room to teach them the whole defense, you need to put the different sub-groups in the same room so they understand how the whole organization works together.

On the other hand, some sub-groups do not need to work together. Just as Ryan doesn't need his offense and defense to work together, you will have some groups that are not interrelated. Define the team as the group of people who need to work together to accomplish the task.

This is a good example of step 9 of *The New Leader's Playbook*: **Secure ADEPT People in the Right Roles and Deal with Inevitable Resistance**

Make your organization ever more ADEPT by Acquiring, Developing, Encouraging, Planning and Transitioning talent:

- **Acquire**: Recruit, attract, and onboard the right people
- **Develop**: Assess and build skills and knowledge
- **Encourage**: Direct, support, recognize, and reward
- **Plan**: Monitor, assess, plan career moves over time
- **Transition**: Migrate to different roles as appropriate

4,379 views May 25, 2011, 12:25pm

How Kenexa CEO Rudy Karsan Is Making the Salary.com Acquisition Work

Former Ernst & Young Partner and Coca Cola CEO Doug Ivester once told me that 30% of acquisitions fail because the acquiring company overpays and saddles itself with unrealistic pro forma plans. They get behind and never catch up. Kenexa CEO Rudy Karsan and his team had no intention of letting that happen to them with their acquisition of Salary.com late last year. Instead, as they reported on May 3, over their first six months, their transition management has them ahead of plan on all the main dimensions.

Karsan knows that financial returns are highly correlated with employee engagement. He explained to me that their studies show that the total shareholder return of the 25 corporations with the highest levels of employee engagement were +18% over the last 15 years as compared to a -4% return for the bottom 25 corporations. Further, employees with effective leadership are six times more engaged than those without effective leadership. There's more on this in Karsan's book We: How to Increase Performance and Profits Through Full Engagement.

Thus, Karsan knew that he had to put effective leadership in place in Salary.com to engage his new employees.

Job #1 is building trust

In many ways, Kenexa's success with Salary.com began earlier in the year when Karsan recruited Zahir Ladhani out of AstraZeneca and put him on Kenexa's bench for six months. This gave Ladhani time to learn Kenexa's culture while waiting for the right assignment.

Salary.com was that assignment. Karsan installed him as the new head of Salary.com and let Ladhani lead the due diligence. This allowed Ladhani to get to know all the key players and practices within Salary.com.

As they got closer to doing the deal, Ladhani picked 4-5 people out of Salary.com to be his core management team. They then used the month between the announcement of the deal and the closing to evaluate all the people. This set them up to tell everyone what their status was on Day one and which of three buckets they fell into:

1 – Stay for 90-120 days to help with the transition. Then exit.

2 – Leave today. (All the finance and G&A people were in this bucket.)

3 – Be part of our team. (200 of the 300 people)

It turned out the lack of games and posturing was a big trust builder.

Job #2 is recognizing people and making them feel appreciated

This had started with the appointment of Ladhani as head. On Day one, Karsan let everyone know that Ladhani spoke with the Kenexa management team's voice. He was Salary.com's people's "last level of appeal". Ladhani then empowered his team and put them to work, recognizing their accomplishments along the way.

Job #3 is acknowledging you're not perfect

Because the "leave today or stay for 90-, 120-day" decisions had been made before the actual acquisition, certain people were let go, including some that should not have been, and Ladhani and Karsan regretted this later. After the acquisition, once they realized their mistake, they brought those individuals back. This happened in 3-4 cases, and most importantly, they had the humility to accept their mistakes and correct them.

Job #4 is growth and learning

Karsan's grandfather in Kenya used to tell him that "*The day you stop learning is the day you start dying. You don't have another choice.*" The same thing is true for organizations. Learning is a core value for Karsan and for Kenexa. He and Ladhani did not make this a choice for the Salary.com people. They needed to adopt the Kenexa culture immediately. From Day one, the Salary.com people that were invited to join the team were treated the same as the rest of Kenexa's employees.

Of course there were some bumps on the road. Certainly the Salary.com people appreciated the firmness of the process. Though some of them would have liked to date before they got married, the results speak for themselves. Of the 200 Salary.com employees invited to be part of the team, Kenexa has lost only 3-4 "A" players. And in their most recent employee engagement survey, six months into the acquisition, the scores of the former Salary.com employees and the rest of Kenexa are "indistinguishable".

This is how effective leadership can accelerate employee engagement and business results and is a good example of Step 1 of *The New Leader's Playbook for Acquisitions*: **Choose how to engage the context and acquired culture.**

Context is a function of the business environment, organizational history and recent business performance, informing the relative importance and urgency of change. Culture underpins "the way we do things here" and is made up of Behaviors, Relationships, Attitudes, Values, and the Environment feeding into readiness for change. Crossing context and culture helps you decide whether to Assimilate, Converge and Evolve (fast or slow), or Shock. Choose your way during the early stages of evaluating a possible acquisition. Then map contributors, detractors, and convincible watchers so you can move each of them one step by altering their balance of consequences.

1,558 views Jun 1, 2011, 11:14am

New Chairman of the Joint Chiefs of Staff Shifts from Commanding to Advising

Image by AFP/Getty Images via @daylife

The man whom President Obama described as *"One of our nation's most respected and combat-tested generals"* will no longer command any troops. In his role as Army Chief of Staff, the entire US Army obeys Martin Dempsey's orders. But in his new role as Chairman of the Joint Chiefs of Staff, he will give up that command authority. Chairman is merely an advisory role. To be fair, this is about as good as it gets as far as advisory roles go in that he will be the president's principal military advisor.

In this role, Dempsey will need to play up his leadership skills around influencing and put his decision-making skills on the back burner. Of course he's the same person he was yesterday, but the context he's operating in is different. Too many leaders fail in new roles because they fail to adjust to changing contexts. This is particularly challenging for someone moving from commanding to advising. Dempsey's move is one example, but this is the situation faced by every CEO managing the transition to non-executive chairman.

Persuasion Framework

Bryan Smith lays out a useful framework of persuasion in "The Fifth Discipline Fieldbook." He suggests five approaches:

TELL is what the combat commander issuing orders in the heat of battle does. There are no discussions. The commander tells. Others obey.

SELL is used by someone trying to persuade someone else that their idea is right, as is

TEST is used by someone looking for a read on the viability of an idea before selling it.

CONSULT is about getting others to help improve an idea.

CO-CREATE happens when people start with a blank page and build the idea together.

No More Orders – Just Advice

In his new role, Dempsey gives up the ability to "Tell." On the one hand, he still has the other four levels of persuasion at his disposal. In his previous positions he most likely used a balance of those approaches. Even though he could, he didn't always tell people what to do.

On the other hand, not having the ability to command changes the context of the other approaches. You are going to be much more open to my selling, testing, consulting, and co-creating if you know I can turn around and tell you what to do if we can't agree. Even when commanders advise, their advice is more equal than others.

But Order Counts

In one sense, all leadership is political. Yet Dempsey's new role is much more political than anything he's been used to – but not political in terms of party politics. As Dempsey's predecessor, Michael Mullen put it in his May 23, 2008 address at the US Naval Academy, the role requires the *"most independent military opinion—neither constrained nor contaminated by personal politics. Part of the deal we made when we joined up was to willingly subordinate our individual interests to the greater good of protecting national interests. The military as an institution must remain a neutral instrument of the state, no matter which party holds sway."*

Dempsey needs to be mindful of the order in which he influences people. Sometimes he'll want to consult with the military commanders before going to Obama and his team. Then his advice to Obama will carry the weight of the full joint chiefs. Other times he'll want to consult with Obama and his team before going to the military commanders. Then his "advice" will carry Obama's weight. In these cases, even if Dempsey can't command, he will be representing people who can.

Influence versus Control

This is a classic example of giving up control to gain influence. Dempsey is giving up control over the army and gaining influence over the nation at its highest levels.

And this is a good example of step 2 of *The New Leader's Playbook*: **Engage the Culture and Your New Colleagues in the Right Context**

Be careful about how you engage with the organization's existing business context and culture. Crossing the need for change based on the context and the cultural readiness for change can help you decide whether to Assimilate, Converge and Evolve (fast or slow), or Shock.

1,227 views Jun 8, 2011, 11:59am

BMW's Focus on Sustainability Drives Record Q1 Profits

Image by AFP via @daylife

BMW earned record profits in the first quarter of 2011, driven by some important choices by CEO Norbert Reithofer, including decisions to focus on what's important, own the things they need to own, and partner with others where and when they can. His actions serve as an excellent example of how CEOs and other senior leaders can make strategic choices which close the gaps between business objectives and the current reality.

Focus on What's Important

Harvard Business School Professor Michael Porter says strategy is choosing what not to do. PrimeGenesis partner Harry Kangis goes one step further:

Choosing not to do something that's a bad idea is easy. The hard choice is choosing not to do something that's a good idea — for someone else.

Reithofer is clear on what's important to BMW, as he discussed during their 2011 annual meeting,

- *To maintain our technological lead in the field of sustainable drive systems with both combustion and electric motors.*
- *To pool the most promising expertise within the company.*
- *To provide customers with attractive mobility services.*

Reithofer rejects the trade-off between sustainability and driving pleasure. As he said in an interview with Spiegel magazine

The concept of premium will be increasingly defined through sustainability in the future. BMW, like no other brand, will still stand for vitality and driving pleasure in the future. But it will also represent efficiency and environmental friendliness.

We have introduced our fuel-saving technology, Efficient Dynamics, as a standard feature in all series. It uses start-stop technology, brake-force energy recovery and other methods to drastically reduce fuel consumption, while at the same providing more power. We call this "Sheer Driving Pleasure 2.0.

Own What They Need to Own

A big part of producing efficient and environmentally friendly cares is achieved through continued investment in the technology of drive systems. They want to be the technology leader and will work to increase profitability to remain independent and stay ahead of Audi and others. At this point, its flagship models are delivering superior experiences to its drivers. BMW's sales reflect this.

They are choosing not to continue on the Formula One race circuit. It's more important to maintain its technical lead in consumer cars than entertainment cars.

Partner With Others

It has chosen to cut staff and reduce spending on components and supplies, partnering with Peugeot as part of its "pooling" strategy – particularly on more environmentally friendly efforts.

Additionally, it has brought in experts to help with the environmentally friendly push. Specifically it has hired a former German foreign minister, Green Party politician Joschka Fischer, and former US Secretary of State Madeleine Albright as advisors to leverage their knowledge and contacts to identify trends early on and manage new emissions laws.

Others trying to navigate our challenging times would do well to take a driving lesson from Reithofer and BMW on how to manage in the context of a rapidly changing environment, hungry competitors and ongoing financial pressures. Record earnings are better than flat tires.

Strategic Choices – Where play? How Win?

At its core, strategy is simply generating and selecting options that will close the gaps between the objectives and current reality. It is about the creation and allocation of resources to the right place, in the right way, at the right time, over time that bring to fruition your mission, vision, objectives and goals while maintaining values.

A simple way to drive strategic choices is by asking two focused questions: Where are we going to play? How are we going to win? Strategy boils down to selecting which options to pursue and which options not to pursue.

This is a good example of step 6 of _The New Leader's Playbook_: **Embed a Strong Burning Imperative**

The burning imperative is a sharply defined, intensely shared, and purposefully urgent understanding from each of the team members of what they are "supposed to do, now." Get this created and bought into early on—even if it's only 90 percent right. You, and the team, will adjust and improve along the way.

4,345 views Jun 15, 2011, 10:31am

Caryn Lerner's 100-Day Action Plan as New CEO of Daffy's

A lesson in overcoming obstacles to jumpstart strategic, operational and organizational processes.

I spoke with Caryn Lerner early on in her tenure as CEO of off-price clothing retailer Daffy's, and then again at the end of the implementation of her new leader's 100-day action plan. While she certainly had her ups and downs, she has managed to make meaningful progress on jumpstarting her strategic, operational and organizational processes.

Background – A 50 year old family-owned, family-run business

Lerner is Daffy's first outside CEO, brought in to turn around declining revenues. Daffy's was filled with long-tenured employees who had been successful "with little or no process, planning and strategy" for years. But that wasn't working any more. In recruiting Lerner, the owners were "very forthcoming" about what they needed, what their issues were "warts and all," what they hoped Lerner would do, what she could not do, and what leadership skills she would need to be successful.

Early days – Relationships and learning

Lerner started even before day one. She learned about the competition in the off-price segment by doing intensive shopping. (There are some members of my family that enjoy intensive shopping perhaps too much. But that's a different story.) She had pre-meetings with the chairwoman, CFO and other board members.

On day one, Lerner met with her new executive team and with Daffy's buyers. Then she had lunch with all the store and other managers. Over the next month she spent more time "observing" than leading, immersing herself in the business. She visited all the stores with the head of stores. She even turned herself into a dress and had herself shipped through the entire distribution chain.

Jumpstarting strategic, operational and organizational processes

To jumpstart her core processes, Lerner brought in some outside experts including:

- Someone out of Saks and Gilt as a consultant to jumpstart Daffy's strategic process with an emphasis on the merchandising strategy
- An HR consultant to jumpstart Daffy's organizational process with a focus on a performance management system, policies and procedures
- The CFO that worked with her in her last job to jumpstart Daffy's operational processes with an emphasis on merchandising planning on a consulting basis

Early Wins

While all this is going on, Lerner worked with her existing management team on a weekly basis to manage the current plan and drive some early wins. So far, Lerner and her team have:

- Opened two new stores
- Taken on new brands that sell for higher price points
- Added event merchandising, starting with Mother's Day
- Added visual merchandising against key trends
- Continued buying 50 percent of its inventory in real time

It's paying off. May was the first time in over a year that Daffy's achieved financial plan!

Lessons from Caryn Lerner's First 100-Days

Lerner both knew where she wanted to take the organization and that she did not have the team in place to get there. So she chose to work with her existing team while supplementing its strength with outsiders. She:

- Got everyone clear on the short-term priorities, while jumpstarting her strategic process
- Put a short-term milestone management system in place, while revamping the overall operating process
- Identified and delivered early wins
- Sorted her team quickly and figured out what moves to make over time
- Drove her communication both in what she said and what she did

This is a good example the value of having your own *New Leader's Playbook*

Leadership is about inspiring and enabling others to do their absolute best together to realize a meaningful and rewarding shared purpose. To that end, three things make a big difference: Get a head start – Manage the message – Build the team.

358 views Jun 22, 2011, 12:00pm

Plum Builders' CEO Rights Roles to Deliver Better Results for Its Customers

Al Giaquinto

Procter & Gamble advertising guru Ken Levy used to say, "Strategy should precede execution." With a copy strategy in place, advertising development works best if the team leverages its leadership skills across a predictable set of steps:

1. Design the ad
2. Agree on the design and budget
3. Produce the ad

When Plum Builders CEO Al Giaquinto started building homes, the game was the same. With a vision/approach in place, home building worked best if the team followed a predictable set of steps:

1. Design the home (Architect)
2. Agree the design and budget (Owner)
3. Produce the home (Builder)

What Al figured out is that this process was isolating the steps of design and construction and was successful only if the person "catching" the plans the architect "threw" over the wall viewed the architect's drawings in the way they were intended. (How many times have you seen projects go askew because the person "catching" your direction didn't interpret them in the way you intended?)

So Al changed the process to an integrated, iterative approach utilizing many of the same concepts that Frank Lloyed Wright used in his organic design approach.

Using this framework the owner, architect and builder openly collaborate on project scope and budget from the start… The architect and builder each have their own area of professional responsibility but accountability to the client for a project that meets budget constraints, design strategy and delivery schedule are prioritized at the start.

The builder's role is to enhance the team with the right players inside and outside his firm: Other design build professionals including pool, landscaping, audio visual, home automation and security, acoustic, and his professionals, an architect, kitchen designer, bath designer, interior designer. The role of building the team by understanding the value each player offers is the key to optimal success."

This has resulted in better satisfied clients and a whole lot less re-work along the way.

Take a hard look at the role sort in your organization

Like Al, we all know how important it is to have the right people in the right roles with the right support. Most see this as an exercise in developing or finding people to fit pre-designed required roles. This is a futile exercise if the roles are wrong to begin with or if the links between the roles are wrong.

Instead, follow these steps:

1. **Commit or re-commit to the mission.** Make sure everyone is clear on what you're trying to accomplish.
2. **Agree on the resources required to accomplish the mission:** financial, human, operational.

3. **Determine the optimal way to manage those resources.** (e.g. architect takes lead on design; builder takes lead on implementation; both coordinating with the owner at every step along the way)
4. **Implement**
5. **Monitor and adjust along the way**. Always checking progress towards the mission with the mission owner.

What's different is the idea of a shared accountability to the mission owner with each functional expert taking the lead in their own area of expertise. This in no way suggests that the experts have to let non-experts tell them what to do. This is all about explicitly coordinating, linking and integrating efforts along the way so that things don't get "thrown "over the wall.

This is a good example of step 9 of *The New Leader's Playbook*: **Secure ADEPT People in the Right Roles and Deal with Inevitable Resistance**

Make your organization ever more ADEPT by Acquiring, Developing, Encouraging, Planning, and Transitioning talent:

- **Acquire**: Recruit, attract, and onboard the right people
- **Develop**: Assess and build skills and knowledge
- **Encourage**: Direct, support, recognize, and reward
- **Plan**: Monitor, assess, plan career moves over time
- **Transition**: Migrate to different roles as appropriate

1,519 views Jun 29, 2011, 11:29am

Job #1 of a Leader: Show Up

Lessons from Chris Christie, Jean-Claude Brizard and Marc Binioff

It was a powerful moment. Late last week, The Today Show's Matt Lauer asked New Jersey Governor Chris Christie what lessons leaders in Washington could learn from New Jersey's recent success in passing a bi-partisan pension bill. Christie replied,

First the President could show up. You can't negotiate through a secondary person. (1)

(Interestingly, this week, President Obama is negotiating directly with Speaker of the House John Boehner and Senate Minority Leader Mitch McConnell.)

You can't lead through a secondary person either. Leadership is about inspiring and enabling others, and ultimately, it's a very personal exercise. As Chicago's new school chief Jean-Claude Brizard gets this. When he

started his previous job as the head of schools in Rochester, NY his vision was to

...create an environment in the district where if he asks a school principal about a specific student and their dreams, aspirations, struggles and achievement, he and school leaders will be able to have a meaningful dialogue about that child's future.(2)

As he moves into his new role in Chicago, <u>Brizard is driving the same message</u>,

It's not about reform for reform's sake, but how do we change the lives of children? That has to be the reason why we do this work.

Salesforce.com CEO Marc Benioff's actions at his annual management off-site meeting also reinforces the need for leaders to engage directly with stakeholders. Benioff invited all 5,000 of Salesforce.com's employees to participate in the meeting virtually and interact in real-time with the management team through their internal social network.

Meaningful dialogue did not start until Benioff himself posted a comment about a presentation while also injecting some humor.(3)

Certainly Christie did not solve his state's budget issues on his own. Brizard doesn't teach students anymore. And Benioff doesn't sell anything himself. But much of what people deep in an organization think they have to do actually gets in the way of their ability to make an impact. These leaders cut through the red tape, change processes, step in, and show up at the critical moment to rally the team and make things happen.

Christie engaged in the debate with other political leaders. He led by doing. Many of Brizard's choices around school employees have been controversial through the years, but no one can doubt his focus on his students. Benioff had a good idea and then modeled the behavior he hoped others would adopt.

While everything communicates, many won't believe what you say. They'll wait to see what you do. When leaders truly believe something is important they don't trust in words alone. They show up - as did the members of the Continental Congress in America 235 years ago this week.

These are all good examples of step 5 of *The New Leader's Playbook*: **Drive Action by Activating and Directing an Ongoing Communication Network (Including Social Media)**

Everything communicates. You can either make choices in advance about what and how you're going to communicate or react to what others do. It is important to discover your own message and be clear on your platform for change, vision, and call to action before you start trying to inspire others. It will evolve as you learn, but you can't lead unless you have a starting point to help focus those learning plans. Identify your target audiences. Craft and leverage your core message and master narrative. Monitor and adjust as appropriate on an ongoing basis.

753 views Jul 6, 2011, 02:54pm

Positive Misdirection Instills Confidence

Image via Wikipedia

It started out as an offer to help find a place for an event. But as Sail to Prevail CEO Paul Callahan got into it, he strengthened his own leadership skills to go beyond the surface and impact people in ways they never expected. And all it took was some positive misdirection.

Understanding that International Federation of Disabled Sailing (IFDS) President Linda Merkle was looking for an event location, Callahan suggested exploring Charlotte Harbor in Florida, and partnered with Merkle to secure local support, assist in planning to raise the funds, as well as help put a logistical plan in place. As a result, IFDS World Championships will be hosted by the Charlotte Harbor Regattas, Inc. in January 2012.

Along the way, Callahan realized why Bridgewater Associates CEO Ray Dalio had been pushing him so hard to focus on the greater impact. Dalio is a major supporter of Callahan's Sail to Prevail, helping fund its mission to create opportunities for disabled children and adults to overcome adversity through therapeutic sailing.

What Callahan finally saw was that the impact goes far beyond the actual sailors and can *"affect very large masses of people"*. Certainly, as Callahan puts it, *"Sailing can be a platform to teach anyone with a challenge to overcome adversity."* In Charlotte County, FL, Callahan and Merkle started with an event. With local support, they used that to rally the community. This is giving members of the community increased confidence, and in turn leading the members of the community to achieve greater meaning in their day-to-day lives.

The positive misdirection was that all the people that thought they were helping others were helping themselves just as much. (By the way, Callahan's own personal story is remarkable. Click here to learn how he overcomes the impossible every day.)

Positive Misdirection with Your Team

There's a powerful model here in moving from event to community to confidence to achievement. In any new leadership position, this model can be used to secure an early team win.

Event

Start with an event you can rally people around. In Callahan's case it was a sailing world championship. In your case it could be onboarding a new employee, launching a new product or deploying a new system. It needs to be an event that is relatively easy for people to understand why you'd want their support.

Community

The first positive misdirection comes with people thinking it's all about the event. It's not. It's about getting them to work together. This can be a first step in bridging towards new behaviors, relationships, attitudes, values, and environment, or a new BRAVE culture.

Confidence

Treat the event like an early win on the way to building a stronger culture. Over-invest in the event to deliver the win. This will give team members greater confidence in themselves as individuals, as a team, and in you as a leader.

Achievement

With that confidence will come greater achievement. As Virgil put it a very long time ago, *"They can because they think they can"*. This is the ultimate misdirection as the event is really just an excuse to get employees to work together in new ways, helping them build confidence and achieve more.

This is a good example of step 8 of _The New Leader's Playbook_: **Over-invest in Early Wins to Build Team Confidence**

Early wins are all about credibility and confidence. People have more faith in people who have delivered. You want your boss to have confidence in you. You want team members to have confidence in you, in themselves, and in the plan for change that has emerged. Early wins fuel that confidence.

455 views Jul 13, 2011, 12:00pm

Are Obama, Boehner, and Cantor going to follow their principles off the cliff?

Image via Wikipedia

"A principle isn't a principle unless it costs you something"

This is one of those quotes that are attributed to all sorts of different people. I heard it from Procter & Gamble's VP of Advertising Bob Goldstein. Others attribute it to Bill Bernbach, one of the founders of the advertising agency DDB. Others attribute it, or a variation on it, to various people they admired along the way. Either way, we're all making tradeoffs between what we want and what we're willing to give up to get it.

We saw two very different examples of this over the past week.

FDIC Head Sheila Bair Fought For the Little Guy

Sheila Bair stuck by her principles even though it severely damaged her relationships with others. As Joe Nocera reports in a terrific article in *The New York Times*, Bair headed up the Federal Deposit Insurance Corporation during the recent financial meltdown. When Nocera asked her what was important, she replied *"Our job is to protect bank customers, not banks."*

She lived by this principle every day in her job. She stood up to any and all comers, including a couple of secretaries of the treasury and other top politicians. Bair was always pushing them to protect the needs of the bank customers and taxpayers, not the banks, not the shareholders, not the bond holders and certainly not the investment banks. As Nocera reports, she would have let Bear Stearns fail to uphold her principles, *"Guess what: Investment banks fail."*

Christian Lopez Gave Back a Gift He Didn't Deserve

Yankee captain and shortstop Derek Jeter had a very good day last Saturday, going five for five and hitting a homerun for his 3,000th hit and then ending the day with a game-winning single. This is merely a milestone in a great career marked by resiliency and sticking with it – two very important characteristics and leadership skills.

Christian Lopez is a fan who attended the game. He ended up with the ball Jeter knocked out of the park for his 3,000 hit. When the Yankees asked what he wanted for the ball, he just gave it to Jeter. As he described it, *"Mr. Jeter deserved it. I'm not gonna take it away from him."* He gave up real money to stick by his principle of doing the right thing.

Which Principles Matter Most?

Messrs. Obama, Boehner, Cantor, and others are wrestling with what imperatives and principles matter most:

- We must fix the economy.
- Those that can, should help those that need.
- No one should spend more than they take in.
- The validity of the public debt of the United States…shall not be questioned.

The issue is that it's hard to do everything at the same time. Assuming all the parties are trying to do the right thing, they still have different perspectives on which right thing is the most important. While Sheila Bair didn't set out to make investment banks fail, she was prepared to pay that cost to protect bank depositors and taxpayers. While Christian Lopez would have liked to own a souvenir baseball, he was not going to take it away from the guy who deserved it.

The leaders of the U.S. government have not set out to default on the country's debt. If refusing to sacrifice other principles leads to that happening, let's just hope they understand the long-term cost of that to present and future generations. A principle isn't a principle unless it costs you something. When that cost is another principle and the future well-being of an entire country, maybe some compromise is warranted.

This is a good example of step 6 of *The New Leader's Playbook*: **Embed a Strong Burning Imperative**

The burning imperative is a sharply defined, intensely shared, and purposefully urgent understanding from each of the team members of what they are "supposed to do, now." Get this created and bought into early on—even if it's only 90 percent right. You, and the team, will adjust and improve along the way.

An absolutely essential part of this is alignment around mission, vision, and values: what you have to get done; what things will look like when you get that done; and the principles you will not give up on along the way – no matter what it costs.

848 views Jul 20, 2011, 11:15am

Three Priorities in Ensuring a Smooth Merger or Acquisition

Susan Salka, President and CEO, AMN Healthcare AMN Healthcare

AMN Healthcare Services CEO Susan Salka says its most recent acquisition of Medfinders is going "exceptionally well." She believes the acquisition has strengthened its position as the country's largest health care staffing company, leading to a doubling of fill rates, keeping more services "in-house", and helping win more business. She's pleased because AMN's customers, leadership and team members now see the benefits of the merger for their businesses and for themselves.

This success did not come without hard work and careful planning. The steps Salka and her team took provide insight into how to use the time before the deal closing to jump-start learning and relationships. Salka built success on a foundation of improved customer service and three priorities:

1. Early conversations with all;
2. A well-resourced Integration Management office;
3. Staying close to the process.

Today In: Leadership

Early Conversations

Salka and her lieutenants had early conversations with AMN's investors and laid out the benefits to its clients and the company culture. Then she spent significant time aligning the combined leadership team, investing heavily in planning and communication between the announcement and the close, and then bringing the combined sales leadership together right after the close. As Salka explained to me,

Investing in planning and communication up front ... so we could have as many decisions made and ready to communicate as possible…That clarity and decisiveness created a lot of trust and reduced anxiety.

Integration Management Office

A merger is not business as usual. AMN established and resourced an Integration Management Office to give it a real-time view of how things were going. As a result, they knew:

- What they were accomplishing and getting done;
- How they were progressing towards their target of adding $10 million in EBITDA;
- How well we were keeping team members motivated and inspired.

Stay Close

Salka learned the importance of communicating with everyone at a personal level to get at their expectations, hopes and fears. It's not good enough to keep tabs on what's going on; leaders must show up. As Salka puts it, you need a management process:

But even more important than that is to be out in the field listening, listening, listening to the team members, to our customers. Because you can hear one thing in a meeting and see it on paper, but if the reality or the perception is different out in the field, whether it be at one of our offices or with a customer, then what's on paper doesn't really matter…You just can't spend enough time out in front of your team members listening – and sharing!

This is a good example of Step 4 of *The New Leader's Playbook for Acquisitions*: **Embrace and Leverage the *Fuzzy Front End* Before the Close.**

The time between knowing you're going to do the acquisition and the deal closing is a gift you can use to get a head start on positioning the acquired leader and team for success. Our experience has shown that those who use this fuzzy front end to put a plan in place, complete their pre-start preparation, and jump-start learning and relationships as much as possible while working towards a deal close, are far more likely to deliver better results faster than those who choose to rest and relax. Five important steps:

1. Identify the most important stakeholders up, across, and down –
    both inside and out.
2. Plan your message, fuzzy front end, and first 100-days.
3. Manage any personal setup for yourself and any people you're
    dropping in so you all have less to worry about after you or they
    start.
4. Conduct pre-start meetings and phone calls as possible to jump-
    start important relationships.
5. Gather information and learning in advance to jump-start learning,
    partly by talking to as many as you can at different levels of the
    acquired organization. They generally know truth.

924 views Jul 27, 2011, 11:53am

What We Can Learn About Negotiating From the Great Compromiser

The chasm seems unbridgeable. While political parties exist partially to keep each other in check, at this point it looks like they are completely thwarting any progress. And progress is essential to keep things from collapsing like a house of cards.

The parties have dug in at the extremes. One wants government to leave it alone so its constituents can do what they do best, build business and wealth leading to work and well-being for others. The other is called to help those that cannot help themselves, firmly believing that a government that will not take care of those that cannot help themselves is abrogating one of its fundamental responsibilities. Neither is prepared to give up anything.

In the middle is one man who understands the path that must be taken to find common ground between the two extremes. As he put it,

I know no South, no North, no East, no West to which I owe allegiance...The union sir, is my country.(1)

The chasm I'm referring to was the chasm between slave and free states. The man in the middle almost two centuries ago was Henry Clay, the American statesman who managed to construct both The Missouri Compromise of 1820 - bringing Maine into the union as a free state to balance the addition of Missouri as a slave state – and the Compromise of

1850 that kept the country from civil war. These helped him earn his reputation as "the great compromiser." It's not unreasonable to believe that Webster was thinking of Clay when he wrote one of his definitions of compromise as "to find a way between extremes."

While Clay drove compromises on Capitol Hill, the steps he used to execute these deals can be applied to those agreements derived in C-suite boardrooms. Qualities of Clay's approach to compromise are reflected in the six-step process featured in our book, "*The New Leader's 100-Day Action Plan.*"

1. **Make a plan**. (Identify the dimensions of the negotiation by answering these questions: What are my needs and concerns? What are others' needs and concerns?)
2. **Get started**. (Identify areas of agreement.)
3. **Clarify positions**. (State, support, and listen.)
4. **Find alternatives**. (The way between the extremes.)
5. **Gain agreement**. (Study proposals, make concessions, summarize, test the agreements.)
6. **Implement**. (Communicate, deliver, and monitor.)

Clay was particularly good at identifying areas of agreement, finding acceptable alternatives and gaining agreement, yet ever mindful of James Russell Lowell's admonition that:

Compromise makes a good umbrella, but a poor roof; it is temporary expedient, often wise in party politics, almost sure to be unwise in statesmanship.

Clay's compromises did not hold over time. Despite everyone's worst fears the house of cards did collapse into civil war. And it was far worse than anyone had imagined.

This is a good example of step 2 of *The New Leader's Playbook*: **Engage the Culture and Your New Colleagues in the Right Context**

Be careful about how you engage with the organization's existing business context and culture. Crossing the need for change based on the context and the cultural readiness for change can help you decide whether to Assimilate, Converge and Evolve (fast or slow), or Shock.

Remember we're all new leaders all the time. We're continually engaging and re-engaging our colleagues to make things happen. As you do, make sure you understand all your stakeholders' needs and concerns, so you can find your way between the extremes and keep your house of cards from collapsing into something that is far worse than anyone imagines.

(1) Speech in Ashland, KY

7,799 views Aug 3, 2011, 11:44am

Procter & Gamble's John Pepper Votes With His Feet

Image by ercwttmn via Flickr

One of the most moving moments of the U.S. Congress's protracted debt ceiling shenanigans was Congresswoman Gabriel Giffords return from her gunshot injuriesto vote. Showing up then communicated how much she cared much louder than anything she could have said.

Former Procter & Gamble (P&G) CEO John Pepper's actions also spoke volumes, reminding his employees that consumers vote with their feet as he voted with his feet. (1) A couple of examples:

Voting with his feet to encourage a young brand manager

I was a young brand manager showing up for work on a typical day. I got into the elevator to go to my office on the 4th floor. Mr. Pepper got in to go to the 11th floor – where the big dogs sat. At the time he was the EVP of the company's entire U.S. operations. I had never spoken to him alone.

Between the 1st and the 4th floors we exchanged greetings and he asked me what I was working on. Then, to my surprise, he got off the elevator with me on my floor to continue the conversation, voting with his feet to show his support. When we were done several minutes later, he asked me to send him a brief write up, which he then circulated as an example of a good initiative.

It's hard to describe how wonderful that made me feel.

Voting with his feet in support of the organization

A couple of years later, there was a P&G annual managers meeting –
13,000 managers in the Cincinnati Coliseum - just after it had been
announced that Ed Artzt was going to be the new CEO and not the man
most had expected, John Pepper.

When Artzt entered the meeting to give his talk, he received a nice round
of applause. When Pepper came out later, he got a nine-and-a-half minute
standing ovation. Every single person in the crowd wanted him to know
how he or she felt.

And then Pepper voted with his feet again by not leaving. Having been
passed over for the P&G CEO slot, he could have gone to all sorts of
places in an instant. But he didn't. He loved P&G and stayed on in the role
the company asked him to fill.

When Artzt's tenure as CEO was over, Pepper got the nod and became
one of P&G's most beloved CEOs ever.

Voting with his feet to help a P&G alum

When we started CEO Connection and its CEO Boot Camps in 2005, the
first person I called to invite to deliver an opening address was John
Pepper. Although he probably didn't remember who I was (the elevator
interaction surely had a greater impact on me than on him), he said yes in
an instant. It didn't matter who I was. He knew that if I had worked at
P&G, I likely shared the same values as he did. And one of those values
was supporting fellow alums. (His talk was wonderful by the way).

This is a good example of step 5 of *The New Leader's Playbook*: **Drive
Action by Activating and Directing an Ongoing Communication
Network (Including Social Media)**

Everything communicates. You can either make choices in advance about
what and how you're going to communicate or react to what others do. It
is important to discover your own message and be clear on your platform
for change, vision, and call to action before you start trying to inspire
others. It will evolve as you learn, but you can't lead unless you have a
starting point to help focus those learning plans. Identify your target
audiences. Craft and leverage your core message and master narrative.
Monitor and adjust as appropriate on an ongoing basis.

John Pepper's communication is consistent. His feet move in sync with his
words. They have to. Both are ruled by his fundamental beliefs.

7,772 views Aug 10, 2011, 11:41am

Be Like Zappos' Tony Hsieh - Answer Three Key Onboarding Due Diligence Questions

Image via Wikipedia

For Zappos CEO Tony Hsieh, the most important decision is where to play. He learned that playing poker. He applied it at Zappos. It's critical for onboarding. In Hsieh's words:

Through reading poker books and practicing by playing, I spent a lot of time learning about the best strategy to play once I was actually sitting down at a table. My big 'ah-ha!' moment came when I finally learned that the game started even before I sat down in a seat.

In a poker room at a casino, there are usually many different choices of tables. Each table has different stakes, different players, and different dynamics that change as the players come and go, and as players get excited, upset, or tired.

I learned that the most important decision I could make was which table to sit at. (1)

40 Percent of New Leaders Fail

40 percent of new leaders fail in their first 18 months. (2) Many of these failures are the result of choosing the wrong table and stepping on an organization, role, or personal land mine that should have been seen before accepting the job.

Three Questions Leading to the Right Table

The ability and willingness to assess and deal with risk is often a critical differentiator between success and failure. Once you've been offered the job—and only after you've successfully dealt with the only three interview questions—do in-depth due diligence to make sure it is right for you. This involves mitigating organizational, role, and personal risks by answering three questions:

1. What is the organization's sustainable competitive advantage? (To get at organizational risk.)
2. Did anyone have concerns about this role; and, if so, what was done to mitigate them? (To get at role risk.)
3. What, specifically, about me, led the organization to offer me the job? (To get at personal risk.)

Organizational Risk

When looking to mitigate organizational risk, be sure to assess risk elements across the 5Cs: Customers, Collaborators, Capabilities, Competitors and Conditions. The good news is that you probably have a significant head start on understanding many of these or you wouldn't even have been considered for the job. But do not rely on what you think you know. Invest the effort to see what new things you can learn. As Christopher Frank and Paul Magnone describe in their book, "*Drinking from the Fire Hose*," pay special attention to what surprised you. In particular, you need to understand all these in the light of the specific job you've been offered.

Role Risk

To mitigate role risk (internal concerns about the role), you should:

- Find the people who had concerns.
- Understand those concerns.
- Understand what has changed to make those concerns go away.
- Believe that those people will support the role (and you) going forward.

In particular, look hard at peers. In general, your new boss and subordinates will understand the role. The most likely place for there to be issues are peers who think your new job overlaps with parts of theirs.

Personal Risk

The goal in mitigating personal risk is to find out if your strengths, motivation and fit are a match for what is required to deliver the expected results. Knowing what you know, would you hire yourself for the job? If there are significant differences, probe and explore and keep the option of walking away open in your mind. Not taking a job due to lack of fit is usually one of the best career moves a leader can make.

Now What?

With those answers in hand, you can then decide if you have a low level of risk that requires no extraordinary actions, manageable risk that you'll manage as you go, mission-crippling risk that you must resolve before going forward, or insurmountable barriers requiring you to walk away.

This is a critical part of step 1 of *The New Leader's Playbook*: **Position Yourself for Success**

There are several components of this including positioning yourself for a leadership role, selling before you buy, mapping and avoiding the most common land mines, uncovering hidden risks in the organization, role, and fit, and choosing the right approach for your transition type.

2,590 views Aug 17, 2011, 12:16pm

In Selling Commodity Products, Zig When Your Competitors Zag

Image by loop oh via Flickr

Plain white paper is the archetypal commodity. But that was just the beginning of the challenge for Finch Paper's VP of Sales and Marketing, Tony McDowell. He had a commodity product at a smaller, regional player, in a declining market. As those 1960s icons of strategy, Cheech and Chong would say, "Bummer, man."

Dig Deep to Identify Areas of Potential Competitive Advantage

McDowell knew he couldn't win by shadowing the big boys. He needed to zig where they were zagging. So he and his team dug deep into the data to find more profitable, growing market segments where their first-in, fast-mover plan would be an advantage.

(This, of course, was what McArthur did in the Pacific – leap-frogging from undefended island to undefended island, bypassing the Japanese army's areas of strength. Since both McDowell and McArthur used it maybe we should call this the McZigZag strategy.)

What the Finch team found was an opportunity to serve emerging digital printing needs across a small set of occasions across a defined set of customer segments. Each opportunity was small enough to require too much flexibility to be attractive to the bigger players; but in the aggregate they comprised an attractive business for Finch.

Build the Capabilities to Win

Winning required three things:

1. The best product for the targeted occasion
2. Operational excellence to deliver the best total cost for customers
3. Customer intimacy to deliver the best total solution for each individual customer

It turns out that not all white paper is the same. Finch developed a specific paper with specific properties, for specific applications and then worked closely with individual   printers to optimize quality results with a lower total print cost.

Then Finch focused its total product supply system to be able to deliver new grades of paper to a relatively small set of customers faster than any other mill.

Then Finch re-aligned its sales and marketing team to allow it to partner with that small set of customers to understand their current and potential needs and co-create solutions that were better than either of them could do on their own.

Win

Finch is not winning everywhere. But that was never the plan. Instead they are winning with some customers, in some segments, for some needs. That was the plan.

This is a good example of step 10 of _The New Leader's Playbook_: **Evolve People, Plans, and Practices to Capitalize on Changing Circumstances**

By the end of your first 100-Days, you should have made significant steps toward aligning your people, plans, and practices around a shared purpose. Remember, this is not a one-time event but, instead, something that will require constant, ongoing management and Darwinian improvement.

In this particular case, McDowell didn't have to look very far into the future to realize that doing the same thing the same way as everyone else was not going to have a happy ending. Instead, the Finch leadership team made some tough choices.

Choosing to zig when everyone else is zagging is not that difficult if everyone else is going in a bad direction. It's a harder choice when you know the zaggers are going in a good direction. As my partner Harry Kangis suggests, the hardest strategic choice is choosing not to do something that's a good idea – for somebody else. This is what's so powerful about Finch's strategy. They are avoiding profitable and popular market segments where they would have just another commodity and focusing on the areas where they can win.

1,345 views Aug 24, 2011, 11:28am

The Power of a Consistent Message Illustrated by WNET's CEO, Neal Shapiro

Image by via @daylife

Every time we were beginning to form up into teams, we would be reorganized. I was to learn later in life that we tend to meet new situations by reorganizing...and a wonderful method it can be for creating the illusion of progress while producing confusion, inefficiency, and demoralization.

Attributed to Petronius Arbiter, d. A.D. 65, Roman governor and advisor (arbiter) to Nero

Reorganizing your people or your ideas is seductive, giving you "the illusion of progress". Don't get me wrong. We're all new leaders all the time. And sometimes reorganizing is exactly the right thing to do. But often, sticking with the same thing for a while gives you and your team the chance to build momentum. Neal Shapiro gives us a good example of that during his tenure as CEO of WNET.

From his very first day in January, 2008, Shapiro has been driving a message of innovation and re-invention. As he puts it,

It's the only way to stay relevant; it's the only way to stay in business…and that has had its challenges since many people have worked here for more than 20 years.

Shapiro's first effort to communicate his message was to create new programs centered around WNET's core strength of arts and culture: two weekly local arts programs--one called Sunday Arts, which features the great museum exhibits, films, galleries and performances going on in New York City, and the other called Reel 13, which airs on Saturday nights and pairs a classic movie with an indie film and a short film created by our viewers. WNET had not truly taken advantage of creating programming to reflect the rich cultural offerings in the city—nor the artistic talent of its viewers.

Other ways he drove his message of innovation and reinvention included:

- Tapping into the trend of **user generated content** and launched a documentary in which viewers sent in video and interviews.
- Taking down the existing website, which had limited video, and replacing it with a **content rich, video centric site** that PBS used as a model to create its own web video player;
- Launching an international news program called World Focus, where Shapiro encouraged **laptop editing**, which saved considerable amounts of money, and more efficient use of partnerships (Associated Press, Al Jazeera and others) to cut down on field reporting expenses;
- Building a two-story studio within Lincoln Center with **cost-efficient robotic cameras** and a set which can be used for many different purposes.

The impact has been meaningful. In March of this year, in response to an RFP from the Governor of New Jersey, Shapiro spearheaded WNET's proposal to take over NJN, the New Jersey state-run television network. Last month, their proposal was accepted and on July 1st, they debuted "NJTV"—their rename of the network—to the citizens of New Jersey.

There have been many changes at WNET during the past 3 years—but Shapiro's core message has remained the same: innovate, reinvent, or go out of business.

The point is not that leaders should say the same thing over and over again. The point is that consistency of core message over time has a multiplier effect. Shapiro brought his message to life with what he did and what he encouraged others to do.

This is a good example of step 5 of _The New Leader's Playbook_: **Drive Action by Activating and Directing an Ongoing Communication Network (Including Social Media)**

Everything communicates. You can either make choices in advance about what and how you're going to communicate or react to what others do. It is important to discover your own message and be clear on your platform for change, vision, and call to action before you start trying to inspire others. It will evolve as you learn, but you can't lead unless you have a starting point to help focus those learning plans. Identify your target audiences. Craft and leverage your core message and master narrative. Monitor and adjust as appropriate on an ongoing basis.

1,450 views Aug 25, 2011, 10:11am

Steve Jobs' Wake Analysis

Image via CrunchBase

You can learn a lot about a manager by the debris he or she leaves in his or her wake. Some managers leave a trail of broken and disillusioned people behind them that never recover from getting run over by the manager. Others leave behind high-performing leaders that go on to do great things.

People working for the best managers perform better when they work for that manager – and after they have done so. See Wake Analysis on People Development Skills for why.

It's a wonderful feeling to plow through time occasionally looking back at the high performing people smiling in your wake. It doesn't happen by accident. You have to decide it's important to you. You have to invest the time and energy to make it happen. Make those choices. A lot of people will thank you. Certainly a lot of people at Apple will be thanking Steve Jobs. See my note on Why Apple is Doing Well Without Steve Jobs for more on how Tim Cook did as interim CEO, suggesting he'll do great as full-time CEO as well.

Steve Jobs' wake analysis will be different than most others'. Steve's vision, risk-taking and follow-through in the pursuit of new and amazing things leaves behind an entire world of people like me whose lives have been measurably improved both rationally and emotionally, all of whom owe Steve a huge debt of thanks.

803 views Aug 31, 2011, 12:28pm

Leadership Lessons from Bloomberg, Christie, Katrina and Irene

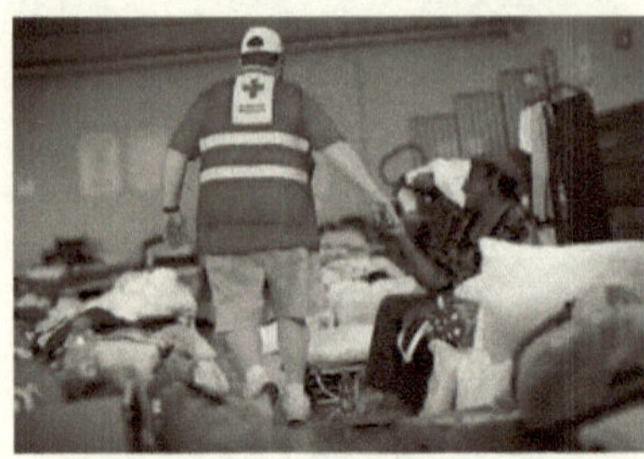

Image by Getty Images via @daylife

I spent the night after Hurricane Irene hit helping out in the Red Cross shelter in Stamford, Connecticut. Six years ago, my sons and I spent a week with a group from our church helping out in New Orleans after Hurricane Katrina hit. Talk about a tale of two cities! As everyone knows, New Orleans' response was marked by its lack of coordination, supplies, direction, and commitment. What we saw this week was a clarity of purpose, strongly coordinated support, flexibility, confidence and commitment.

THE MICRO VIEW

At our shelter in Stamford this week, everyone helping out kept their eyes on the people in need. No one was worrying about whose job something was or was not. Everyone was worrying about how to make a very bad situation better for the people in need. As the Red Cross's Charley Shimanski says, we were the best part of these people's worst day.

The coordinated support was remarkable as well. At the shelter were a handful of volunteers from the Red Cross, a member of the Stamford department of health, a nurse and building maintenance. Throughout the very long, dark night we had periodic visits from fire and police staffs, offering a cheering smile and any support they could provide. Additionally, others' support was entirely visible. The Salvation Army had prepared meals. Other organizations had dropped off supplies and equipment.

THE BROADER VIEW

We learn this lesson over and over again in crises, in disasters, in day-to-day events: preparation breeds confidence. A little over-preparation, a little over-communication, a little over-anticipation goes a long way.

I personally like the "How stupid would you feel" test. When faced with tough decisions, how stupid would you feel if you ordered a few too many people to evacuate and a couple of them were inconvenienced? How stupid would you feel if you ordered a few too few people to evacuate and they got into serious trouble. Mayor Bloomberg in NYC, Governor Christie in NJ, other governors up and down the East Coast applied this test early and often this past week and minimized the numbers seriously affected.

THE LEARNING VIEW

A lot went well this past week. And as one of the people who is still without power, I can tell you a lot could have gone better. Either way, there are some lessons that apply. Generally speaking, our leaders did a better job this week than six years ago during Hurricane Katrina in:

1. Preparing in Advance
2. Reacting to Events
3. Bridging the Gaps

Those of you that have read my paper on "Leading through a Crisis – A 100-Hour Action Plan" will recognize those three ideas. Those of you that have not read it can either send me an email to request it at gbradt@primegenesis.com or go through it in the appendices of the third edition of our book "The New Leader's 100-Day Action Plan" when it comes out in October. The main points are:

1) **Prepare in advance.** The better you have anticipated possible scenarios, the more prepared you are, the more confidence you will have when crises strike. Homeland Security, FEMA, the Red Cross, state governors, mayors and others were better prepared this time around and it showed.

2) **React to events.** The reason you prepared is so that you all can react quickly and flexibly to the situation you face. Don't over-think this. Do

what you prepared to do. Local responders reacted well this time around, continually adjusting to the ever-evolving situations they faced.

3) **Bridge the gaps**. In a crisis, there is inevitably a gap between the desired and current state of affairs. Rectify that by bridging those gaps in the:

- **Situation**: Implementing a response to the current crisis.
- **Response**: Improving capabilities to respond to future crises.
- **Prevention**: Reducing the risk of future crises happening in the first place.

This is a good example of step one of *The New Leader's Playbook*: **Position Yourself for Success**

There are several components of this including positioning yourself for a leadership role, selling before you buy, mapping and avoiding the most common land mines, uncovering hidden risks in the organization, role, and fit, and choosing the right approach for your transition type.

9,724 views Sep 7, 2011, 11:55am

GE CEO Jeff Immelt's Long-term View 10 Years In

Image by General Electric via CrunchBase

Some leaders obsess over daily sales. Some track monthly milestones. Some focus on quarterly profits. General Electric's (GE) Jeff Immelt thinks in terms of decades.

Today marks Immelt's 10th anniversary as CEO of GE. For most CEOs, surviving a decade in the job is a pipe dream. (Recall, 40 percent of new leaders fail in 18 months). For Immelt, 10 years is probably the halfway point.

Much has been written about what he and GE have done well and less well over that decade (see articles in Reuters, Fortune and The Wall Street Journal). And Immelt will forever be compared to his predecessor, Jack Welch. But Immelt is clear that he wants to be judged not on what he accomplished in his first decade in the job, not on what he accomplishes in two decades in the job, but on his lasting contributions to GE over time – over a long time.

Three Priorities: Strategy, Culture, People

Earlier this year, Immelt told blogger Neville Medhora that he sees his main job as CEO to *"Pick initiatives and businesses to get involved in, shape the company culture, pick great people."*

Interestingly, Welch told Warren Bennis something similar in 1999 about his job as CEO: *"Selecting the right people, allocating capital resources, and spreading ideas quickly."*

Strategy

Strategy is about the creation and allocation of the right resources, to the right place, in the right way over time. Whether you call it "allocating capital resources" or picking the "initiatives and businesses to get involved in," the heart of strategy is choices around where you want to play and how you want to win over whatever timeframe is important to you.

In his last earnings call, Immelt gave us a little insight into his timeframe when he talked about Aviation and how he's looking "*at the position GE has, not just for a year or two, but for a decade.*" (1)

This is not a throwaway line. The strategic choices a leader makes with a one- or two-year horizon are different than the choices a leader makes who's looking out a decade into the future.

Culture

There's a subtle difference in the way Immelt is steering GE's culture from the way Welch did. While they are both passionate about "spreading ideas quickly," Immelt is pushing decisions down and out.

He has to. When he took over, two thirds of GE's revenue was in the U.S. Now, the majority of it is outside the U.S. He's moving his senior leaders out into the field, like Vice Chairman John Rice in Hong Kong. Immelt wants a culture of local decision making fueled by senior leaders in place locally with the knowledge and skills to make the right decisions.

People

GE has long been a source of strong general managers. That's still important. Now Immelt is putting a premium on deep functional and business knowledge as well.

Do you remember the old description of the difference between a generalist and a specialist? A generalist is someone who knows less and less about more and more until eventually he or she knows nothing about everything. On the other hand, a specialist is someone who knows more and more about less and less until eventually he or she knows everything about nothing. Obviously, both are useless.

The right answer lies somewhere in between: general managers with deep functional and business knowledge.

This is a good example of step 10 of *The New Leader's Playbook*: **Evolve People, Plans, and Practices to Capitalize on Changing Circumstances**

By the end of your first 100 days, you should have made significant steps toward aligning your people, plans, and practices around a shared purpose. Remember, this is not a one-time event but, instead, something that will require constant, ongoing management and Darwinian improvement.

Immelt is a model for long-term, ongoing management and Darwinian improvement. Just as he is viewing the first 100 days of his 11th year in the job as the first 100 days of the rest of his career, so should all of us. Like Immelt, we're all new leaders all the time.

718 views Sep 11, 2011, 08:46am

Which Way to Run? Lessons from 9/11 Choices

Image via Wikipedia

The fight or flight instinct is one of our most basic survival tools. Everyone was running on 9/11. Most ran away from trouble. The heroes ran toward it. And the leaders helped others run in the most appropriate direction.

Make no mistake about it. The first responders and their leaders displayed a selfless courage that most of us can only dream about. Our world is a better place because people like them existed and continue to exist. We desperately need fire, police, emergency medical, military and other personnel that will put themselves in harm's way to protect others.

There were other leaders as well. Though they may have been unnoticed and unsung, they helped others in their flight away from danger. We need them just as much as we need those leading others into harm's way.

And then there were those leading the leaders. New York Mayor Rudy Giuliani knew that people were going to watch what he did far more than they were going to listen to what he said. So he went down to the site. He calmed the panic. And then he followed up – relentlessly – attending hundreds of funerals for 9/11 victims. To be clear, Giuliani has his flaws and detractors. He is far from perfect – as are we all. But in a time of crisis and panic, he led by example and made a huge impact. As he told Steve Forbes in a recent interview during which Rudy Giuliani recalls the first moments of September 11th, 2001:

I always had a firm rule that, as best I could, if I was going to have to make decisions about an emergency, I better go there, observe it, see it, then I'd know what advice to rely on and what advice not to....

I always try to calm down the overexcited people, because I think that emotion gets in the way of thinking.

The lesson is that we need all sorts of leaders: those that will lead others into harm's way, those that will lead others out of harm's way, and those that will lead the leaders. Whichever way you choose to lead, remember that everything communicates: what you say, what you do, what you don't say, what you don't do, and which way you run.

1,993 views Sep 14, 2011, 03:20pm

Intuit's Current and Former CEO Drive Value Proposition In Sync

Image via Wikipedia

As Intuit CEO Brad Smith puts it, *"Strategies alone don't move mountains. Bulldozers do."* Smith and former Intuit CEO Scott Cook were together on last week's earning's call. That in itself is remarkable because Cook stepped down as CEO in 1994. Yet he's still involved, passionate about the business and working everyday with a focus on *"creating a solution where there has been not one."* (1)

Intuit's Value Proposition

Smith and Cook are together on Intuit's value proposition as well. Their digital tax products have garnered higher Net Promoter Scores than their main competitors (tax stores) and are sold at a much lower price point (around 75 percent less). Creating a better solution is good. Delivering it less expensively is valuable. Recall, this was one of the main planks of Sam Martin's efforts at A&P as well.

Smith and Cook are together on what their bulldozers need to do and how they need to do it. Smith's full bulldozer quote is *"Strategies alone don't move mountains. Bulldozers do. And that's where execution and a set of rigorous financial principles also come into play."* Strategy is theoretically elegant and practically useless until it becomes strategy in action.

Finally, Smith and Cook are together on the importance of agility. If you scan through what they've said through the years, it keeps reappearing:

"No team is bigger than two pizzas can feed" – Smith on Bloomberg TV

"Leadership by experiment… (instead of) politics, persuasion, and PowerPoint" – Cook at Intuit's leadership conference

"Got to go from idea to end market in less than six weeks" – Smith on Bloomberg TV

A Clear, Consistent Strategy

Intuit has a clear, ongoing imperative to help people manage their financial lives and help them save time and be more productive doing so. That imperative is driven in sync by its original founder and current CEO. Now, just as Cook is letting Smith drive the main bulldozer, Smith is letting others drive their own bulldozers and experiment their way to success.

Part of Intuit's ongoing success has to be attributed to the clarity and consistency of its strategy and way of working. People working there know what they are expected to do and how they are expected to do it.

Another factor in its success is still having Cook around. Well into the 1980s, people at the Walt Disney Company asked "What does Walt want?" It was a good way to keep in touch with the founder's vision, even though Walt died in 1966. At Intuit, people stay in touch with the founder's vision by interacting with the founder himself. There's no doubt that Brad Smith is in sync with that value proposition.

Make sure you're getting the full lesson here about what makes for strong burning imperative. The best are:

- **Customer-focused**, drive a customer-relevant value proposition
- **Sharply defined** and crystal clear to all
- **Intensely shared** by all – across the generations
- In sync with the organization's **purpose** and founder's intent
- As **urgent** today as they were when they were originally drafted
- **Continually evolving** through experimentation as the team adjusts and improves along the way
- **The engine** that powers executional bulldozers

This is a good example of step 6 of *The New Leader's Playbook*: **Embed a Strong Burning Imperative**

The burning imperative is a sharply defined, intensely shared, and purposefully urgent understanding from each of the team members of what they are "supposed to do, now." Get this created and bought into early on—even if it's only 90 percent right. You, and the team, will adjust and improve along the way.

Get your imperative in place. And then leverage it across your team and organization with the appropriate combination of relentless discipline and agile leadership.

922 views Sep 21, 2011, 01:10pm

The Los Angeles Urban League's Blair Taylor Follows the Only Possible Path to Success

There is a strong argument to be made that an organization's culture is its only truly sustainable competitive advantage. Plans can be duplicated. People leave. Processes atrophy. Even patents expire. Cultures endure.

When Blair Taylor became CEO of the Los Angeles Urban League in 2005, he took over an organization with an 80-plus year history of success helping African-Americans and other minorities in Los Angeles achieve economic self-reliance, parity, power and civil rights. And he took over from John Mack, a strong leader who had led the League for 36 years. This was an organization whose behaviors, relationships, attitudes, values and environment were set – and working. (Follow this link for more on the BRAVE cultural framework from the new 3rd edition of *The New Leader's 100-Day Action Plan*.)

But the world was changing **and the League would need to change too** if it was going to make the impact it needed to have on its community going forward. Taylor knew that the only possible path to success was for him to converge into the existing culture and evolve it by standing on the shoulders of the giants that had come before him.

Taylor spent a lot of time getting to know all the critical stakeholders. When he was done, he went back and spent more time getting to know them even better. As just one example, he continues to have lunch with one board member or community leader a week. There are 40 board members and literally dozens of community leaders. So when he completes the last lunch, he goes back and starts all over again, and again, and again.

From rescue to systemic change

The fundamental evolution Taylor is leading is from a rescuer model (primarily through training minorities for better jobs) to holistic, systemic change. Taylor is leading the Organization to go neighborhood by neighborhood and focus on improving five things: **safety, education, health, employment, housing**, with community engagement from the bottom-up as the backdrop for sustainable systemic change. Improving those betters the quality of life for the people in those neighborhoods.

It's not just that the five things are interrelated. The challenge is that changing those five requires the work of a whole network of partner agencies. The League partners with something like 170 different agencies in its work. Each is important. Each is focused. All are stronger together than any is on its own.

Another challenge is that the communities are often wary of others trying to change them. Too many times they feel like they were duped by people coming in from the outside with a solution, implementing it, and then going away before it really took root. Too many times they saw through the hidden agendas of their "helpers" to take more than they give. And the communities have power. You don't have to believe me. Just ask Walmart how it felt when Inglewood's community leaders literally ran it out of town.

This is where the League's history comes into play. Because the League has been a part of the communities for almost 90 years at this point, communities believe it will stick around. This gives the League the license to try. And then, as the results start with crime going down (safety), graduation rates improving (education), healthcare improving, employment rising, and housing improving, the communities get behind the efforts. And that, of course, is the cultural change that Taylor and the Los Angeles Urban League are most excited about making.

This is a good example of step 2 of _The New Leader's Playbook_: **Engage the Culture and Your New Colleagues in the Right Context**

Be careful about how you engage with the organization's existing business context and culture. Crossing the need for change based on the context and the cultural readiness for change can help you decide whether to Assimilate, Converge and Evolve (fast or slow), or Shock.

What Taylor is doing that is so remarkable is the long-term approach he's taking to two cultural changes simultaneously.

1.   He has taken his time converging into the Los Angeles Urban League culture, cherishing the legacy of his predecessors, treasuring each and every board member, outside supporter, and knowledge-filled employee.
2.   He is taking a cultural transformation approach to the neighborhoods and communities the League is in business to help. He knows that rescuing individual people, implementing short-term plans, fixing discrete processes can never have the long-term sustainable impact that comes from changing a culture for the better.

26,956 views Sep 23, 2011, 08:00am

Meg Whitman's Day One Itinerary as CEO of Hewlett-Packard

Image by Getty Images via @daylife

Everything is magnified on any CEO's first day. If being CEO is like living in a fishbowl (which it is), day one is the day when the lights are turned up full and everyone gathers around the bowl for their first glimpse into the future.

But, given all that's happened at Hewlett-Packard (H.P.) over the past several years, that analogy doesn't even begin to depict the scrutiny that Meg Whitman is going to receive as she onboards on her first day as its new CEO. (Follow this link for more on why Whitman's predecessor, Leo Apotheker joined the 40% of senior executives that fail in their first 18 months)

Everything Whitman says, everything she does, everything she doesn't say and everything she doesn't do will get dissected, bisected, trisected, and pieced back together by all sorts of different people in all sorts of different ways. Thus, it is especially important that Whitman take control of day one and keep several things in mind.

1) It is personal. As the CEO, Whitman will have a huge impact on H.P. employees' lives. These people will try hard to figure out her, and her potential impact, as soon as they can. They may even rush to judgment.

2) Order counts. Whitman needs to be circumspect about the order in which she meets with people and the timing of when she does what throughout day one and her first week.

3) Messages matter. Whitman staked out her message in her first press conference:

Deliver the world-class products, solutions, and services our customers have come to expect from H.P.… to get H.P. back on track.

Even in a tough turnaround situation like this, Whitman needs to have a bias toward listening. As Mark Hubbard, one of my business partners used to say, "no one cares how much you know until they know how much you care." Whitman may not have done a perfect job connecting with people during her campaign for governor of California. She needs to really focus on connecting with people at H.P.

4) Location counts. Whitman needs to think about where she will show up for work on day one. Hint: it shouldn't be her designated office by default.

5) Signs and symbols count. Whitman must be aware of all the ways in which she communicates, verbally and nonverbally. Think <u>BRAVE: Behaviors, Relationships, Attitudes, Values and Environment</u>. In her case, H.P.'s people are going to be on the lookout for a couple of things in particular:

- Trust and respect for individuals

- Focus on a high level of achievement and contribution

- Uncompromising integrity

- Achieving common objectives through teamwork

- Flexibility and innovation

(By the way, these five are the core components of <u>the HP way</u>.)

6) Timing counts. Day one does not have to match the first day Whitman gets paid or the day after she is announced. Whitman should decide which day she wants to communicate as day one to facilitate other choices about order and location.

This is a good example of step 4 of _The New Leader's Playbook_: **Take Control of Day One: Make a Powerful First Impression**

Everything is magnified on Day One, whether it's your first day in a new company or the day your new role is announced. Everyone is looking for hints about what you think and what you're going to do. This is why it's so important to seed your message by paying particular attention to all the signs, symbols, and stories you deploy, and the order in which you deploy them. Make sure people are seeing and hearing things that will lead them to believe what you want them to believe about you and about themselves in relation to the future of the organization.

4,827 views Sep 28, 2011, 08:00am

True Value Hardware Deploys Three Keys to Successful Culture Change

Image by --Mike-- via Flickr

Lyle Heidemann knew exactly what he needed to do when he took over as CEO of True Value Hardware in 2005: shift the organization's focus from wholesale excellence to retail expertise.

In an effort to save money, the organization spent the three years before Heidemann took over as CEO tightly managing costs, which included headcount reductions. Despite these actions, the company did not achieve its sales or profit forecasts. As Heidemann recently explained to me, it was time to help its retailers accelerate growth:

We are a wholesale company owned by our retailers…We needed to change our focus from figuring how to get (our retailers) to buy something from us to helping them sell to the ultimate customer…from a wholesale focus to a retail focus. Our vision, our strategy and our mission all follow.

The challenge was <u>changing the organization's culture</u> so that its behaviors, relationships, attitudes, values and environment all helped every True Value be the best hardware store in town Heidemann knew in advance that this was going to be a five-year effort. And he knew he would have to do it in stages. Six years in, we know he was right. Now the "vast majority" of True Value's associates buy-in to the strategy and are focused on helping its retailers grow.

The key steps Heidemann deployed included:

- **Preparing** management and associates by getting them aligned around the end game;
- **Implementing** the changes through the co-op's retail members;
- **Following through** with ongoing, consistent communication.

(Note these are steps that could have helped Time Inc.'s Jack Griffin keep from failing in a similar situation as described in this article on "<u>When a Shock Fails</u>".)

1) Prepare

Heidemann first concentrated on getting his eight direct reports to commit to the vision and the need to change the culture. There were individuals who felt uncomfortable with changing the focus, and recognized this would require personal risk-taking on their part and a number of years of dedicated commitment. As a result, all did not make the journey.

Defining the end game is always the hardest part.

Then Heidemann and his management team turned their attention to the top 75 leaders in the organization, getting them to buy-in to the change and the approach. These first two steps took several months. Even with a great sense of urgency and a clear platform for change, no leader can change the culture on his or her own. It's always worth the time to build the team up front.

These were the people that manage the people.

Heidemann and his leadership team then enrolled everyone else. They conducted monthly "forums" to share the big picture (not the detail) and engage the associates in ongoing conversations. The turning point came when he bussed the headquarter associates out to a warehouse they'd set up with the new retail store format. He and his leadership team said, "We could be this. This is what retail is. This is our point of view."

Now they were listening.

2) Implement

This had to be an evolution, not a revolution. In a co-op, the central group can't tell the members what to do. But it can give them new tools and show them how much better their business could be if they adopted the tools. This is what Heidemann and his ever-growing band of supporters did and continue to do in their "markets," round-tables and weekly communication.

We're dependent on helping our retailers grow.

3) Follow through

It's ongoing. Heidemann continues to spend time with retailers at the store level. He's visited over 1,000 stores. He knows their issues. He knows their results. He's conducted 14 roundtables with retailers in just the last three months. Heidemann and his team continue to drive change at every level, from the back room to the shelf, from the headquarters to the mom and pop hardware store that is the hub of the community.

The messaging has been consistent…If you get the people that manage the people committed to change, the people that work for them over time will change with you.

This is a good example of step 5 of *The New Leader's Playbook*: **Drive Action by Activating and Directing an Ongoing Communication Network (Including Social Media)**

Everything communicates. You can either make choices in advance about what and how you're going to communicate or react to what others do. It is important to discover your own message and be clear on your platform for change, vision, and call to action before you start trying to inspire others. It will evolve as you learn, but you can't lead unless you have a starting point to help focus those learning plans. Identify your target audiences. Craft and leverage your core message and master narrative. Monitor and adjust as appropriate on an ongoing basis.

(Follow this link for more on a new model for communicating in today's world.)

The lesson to learn from True Value's transformation is the power of a consistent message and the importance of driving that message all the way through the organization over and over again over time. Six years in, Lyle Heidemann is still treating every day like the first day of the rest of his career.

1,203 views Oct 5, 2011, 08:20am

Despite Bleak Housing Market, Toll Brothers CEO Isn't Panicking

Image via Wikipedia

Put yourself in Doug Yearley's shoes in November 2009. You've just been named EVP on the way to becoming CEO of luxury home builder Toll Brothers, a company that lost $750 million in the year that just ended due to accounting write downs. You're entering the fifth year of a recession in your industry. Your core revenues were down 44 percent versus the prior year, and 75 percent versus the peak a few years before. If there was ever an organization that required significant change, this was it. Right?

Wrong.

Yearley had to engage this culture and his colleagues in the right context. Doug knew three things as he transitioned into his role as the second CEO ever at the company:

1. The organization was strong. It had cash in the bank and solid processes in place, including a long-standing management review every Monday evening.
2. He was an integral part of that organization. Yearley had been there for 20 years and steadily progressed as a leader. At the point he took over from Robert Toll as CEO in June 2010, he had spent 800 Monday evenings with Robert on those management calls.
3. He knew what he could control, and what he could not control, and was confident that Toll would come through the dark days and emerge stronger.

Two years later, it looks like they are weathering the storm. Even though the housing market is still bleak, Toll just announced it fifth straight quarterly profits. As Yearley is quick to point out, not enough profits – but they are profits. They have $1.2 billion of cash and $800 million in available credit.

Yearley, Robert Toll and their team are doing a couple of things right.

Face the brutal truths head on

First, they are facing the brutal truths head on. As Yearley explained to me, *"This incredibly deep and dark housing recession is like none we've ever seen before."* They are continually "right sizing" where they have to, centralizing purchasing and watching incentives. They are managing cash carefully. Delivering even small profits with revenues down 75 percent is no mean trick.

Position yourself for future success

Second, they are positioning themselves to take advantage of the upturn when it comes. As Yearley told me,

Because we have a strong cash position and balance sheet…I can challenge the company to look into new ideas…This keeps it exciting for people even though sales may not be where we want them to be.

Those ideas include:

- Continuing their push into urban (started in 2003 – 22 percent of their revenues now come from high-rises in NYC)
- Looking at international opportunities
- Establishing Gibraltar Capital to buy distressed portfolios of loans
- Looking at new markets within the United States

What Doug did not do was panic. He did not shock the system. He's confident that he and his team can continue to right size the company, grow and return to meaningful profitability.

This is a great example of step 2 in The New Leader's Playbook: **Engage the Culture and Your New Colleagues in the Right Context**

Be careful about how you engage with the organization's existing business context and culture. Crossing the need for change based on the context and the cultural readiness for change can help you decide whether to Assimilate, Converge and Evolve (fast or slow), or Shock.

Context is a function of the business environment, organizational history and recent business performance, informing the relative importance and urgency of change. Culture underpins "the way we do things here" and is made up of Behaviors, Relationships, Attitudes, Values, and the Environment feeding into readiness for change. Crossing context and culture helps you decide whether to Assimilate, Converge and Evolve (fast or slow), or Shock. Choose your way. (Follow this link for more on context and culture.)

In this case, the business environment was beyond ugly. Recent business performance was terrible. But the organization's history and competitive position trumped those issues. A less well-informed leader might have been tempted to change too many things too fast. Not Doug Yearley.

3,717 views Oct 12, 2011, 01:04pm

Steve Jobs and the Power of a Passionate Focus

Image by @boetter via Flickr

Focus. This article is about the power of focus. The key takeaway is the need to drive a message you are passionate about against as few points as possible, and ideally one main, overriding imperative. In this case, focus. Clear?

It's a lesson reinforced by Steve Jobs, Bill Clinton, JK Rowling, and others.

Jobs

In Steve Job's 2005 commencement speech at Stanford, he told three stories to make three points:

1.   Follow your heart
2.   Don't settle
3.   Don't live someone else's life

In one way or another, all three points communicate the same thing: figure out what's really important, what's in your heart, in your imagination, your passion. Put all your energy into overcoming the obstacles you can, accepting the things you must, and connecting with those that matter. Focus.

As has been written about by a whole range of individuals in the week since Jobs' death and felt by most of the people on the planet in one way or another, the man's passionate focus on what he thought was really important changed the world for the better for all of us.

Clinton

1992. Bill Clinton is campaigning against the first George Bush. His lead is starting to slip. What does he do? He returns to his three main campaign points "Change vs. more of the same. The economy, stupid. Don't forget healthcare." Of these, what is most remembered is "The economy, stupid." That's his focus because that's what was most cared about. It's a Maslow's hierarchy sort of thing. If people can't afford food and shelter, they can't move on to the next things. (Plus ca change....)

Whether or not you agree with his policies, you have to admire what Clinton was able to accomplish through the power of focus. Whether or not he really cared, he certainly made us believe he did.

Rowling

In JK Rowling's 2008 commencement speech at Harvard, she focused on two points:

1. The value of failure
2. The power of imagination

It's another great example of the same point – and well worth watching. When Rowling hit rock bottom, she stripped away everything else and focused on what she was most passionate about. Both her and Jobs imagined new worlds. Both made a huge impact.

Focus

All my learning as a leader myself, from working with leaders going into new roles, and from interviewing leaders for this column, makes me believe that

- focusing on one burning imperative rallies the team
- delivering one early win gives the team confidence
- driving one over-riding message improves communication

There is real power in focusing as much of your energy on the one thing you care most about. Figure out what's important. Manage the distractions. Focus.

Embed a Strong Burning Imperative is the pivotal step 6 of _The New Leader's Playbook_.

The burning imperative is a sharply defined, intensely shared, and purposefully urgent understanding from each of the team members of what they are "supposed to do, now." Get this created and bought into early on—even if it's only 90 percent right. You, and the team, will adjust and improve along the way.

It starts with you. Make sure you're focusing your own and your team's efforts on the one most important imperative you are most passionate about.

1,892 views Oct 19, 2011, 08:45am

JPMorgan CEO Jamie Dimon's Public Lambasting of the Bank of Canada

Image by Getty Images via @daylife

In last week's *Financial Times'* "Judgment Call" section, JPMorgan CEO Jamie Dimon's public lambasting of the Bank of Canada was highlighted and a panel of experts was asked to weigh in on whether it's best to wage such debates publicly or "more quietly." I suggested that the choice is not so much either or, but which when. The key is the target audience. Executives must be clear about whom they are trying to influence, and when and how to do that directly and indirectly.

Communication is a critical leadership skill because everything communicates: what leaders say, do, don't say, don't do, and *where* they say and do it. The most effective leaders do three things prior to communicating:

1. Identify Target Audiences

There is rarely one single target audience. Instead, it's important to influence the target directly and to influence their influencers. Beyond conversing with bank regulators, Dimon also knew he had to connect with the public to influence the regulators. As a result, he took his argument public to do so.

2. Craft an Overarching Message and Key Communication Points

Great communication pivots off of a central message. Great examples of this include, *"We're going to be ranked one or two or we're going to get out,"* one of Jack Welch's early messages at General Electric, and *"A car in every driveway*," Henry Ford's overarching message deployed in the early twentieth century. Dimon has a relentless focus on truth as a way to manage risk. The overarching message anchors the communication plan. Your communications points both flow from this message and reinforce it.

3. Choose the Most Appropriate Media

The explosion of new social media forums was the main catalyst for us removing what we wrote about communications in the first two editions of our book, " *The New Leader's 100-Day Action Plan* ," and starting fresh in the third edition. Social media should make you re-think everything you know about where to communicate. If you don't believe me, there are a couple of Middle Eastern ex-dictators who can reinforce the point.

This is why the choice is not about which media to deploy and not deploy, but when to deploy them. Ignoring any media is merely ceding your ability to influence the audience engaging with that media. The conversations will always continue with or without you.

Following these three steps leaders must then implement a series of conversations across targets and media, monitoring and adjusting along the way. This is why it was important for Dimon to take his arguments public and influence the influencers.

This is a good example of step 5 of *The New Leader's Playbook*: **Drive Action by Activating and Directing an Ongoing Communication Network (Including Social Media)**

Everything communicates. You can either make choices in advance about what and how you're going to communicate or react to what others do. It is important to discover your own message and be clear on your platform for change, vision, and call to action before you start trying to inspire others. It will evolve as you learn, but you can't lead unless you have a starting point to help focus those learning plans. Identify your target audiences. Craft and leverage your core message and master narrative. Monitor and adjust as appropriate on an ongoing basis.

217 views Oct 26, 2011, 02:07pm

Ron Krueck's Vision of a More Welcoming Michigan Avenue Facade in Chicago

The Spertus Institute for Judaic Studies in Chicago faced a challenge. It was a wonderful place for people to come together to learn from each other and share perspective on Judaic history, culture and issues in lively discourse. But its building sent a different message. It said, *"We're special. Don't even think about coming in here unless you've been invited."*

The good news was that the Institute owned a vacant lot next door to its building on Michigan Avenue in Chicago. The bad news was that it was right in the heart of an historic district, so it was severely limited in the renovations it could consider.

This was when it brought in the architecture firm Krueck + Sexton.

Ron Krueck took this project to heart and worked to find a way to make Spertus' building more welcoming, while also appealing to the powers that controlled the historic district.

- First, he looked at a stone façade. That fit with the district, but was, well, cold.

- Then he looked at different materials to create curves. That was a little more interesting, but hard to model.

- Finally, he turned the curves into a faceted design. This was a way to keep the welcoming aspects of the curves in a way that they could actually craft in a model.

The Institute's director, Howard Sulkin, loved it.

The new building changed the face of the Institute. Now it welcomes people in and communicates the organization's values of openness, transparency and hospitality.

Iterating towards a vision

As Ron Krueck explained to me, getting to his vision of the building was an iterative process.

We started with several different materials because of the context," Krueck said. But they were getting in the way of the design. So we evolved into a more and more glass building. We started with something that was more undulating. The breakthrough was one morning when we were presenting some concepts of new composition. Because of the ease of making the models, we triangulated the curved surfaces…Howard came in and immediately said 'that's it'.

When we finally presented it, the historic board was enthusiastic. It didn't want a mock historic building. It saw this as part of the continuum of the past, present and future of the district.

It's about their vision, not yours

"Vision" is one of those overused words that means different things to different people. Leaders are expected to have a vision. Sometimes it's not clear where they are supposed to get their visions from.

Ron Krueck needed a way to solve his client's problem. His vision did not come to him in a dream. Instead, he had to build it up step-by-step through a process of experimenting and failing, and then doing it all over again.

Don't think your vision needs to come about instantaneously. Some visions need time and space to percolate. Perhaps most importantly, remember that the key is not the vision that you see as the leader, but the vision you help others see. Leadership is all about inspiring and enabling others. A compelling vision is a critical part of an inspiring imperative.

This is a good example of step 6 of _The New Leader's Playbook_: **Embed a Strong Burning Imperative**

The burning imperative is a sharply defined, intensely shared, and purposefully urgent understanding from each of the team members of what they are "supposed to do, now." Get this created and bought into early on—even if it's only 90 percent right. You, and the team, will adjust and improve along the way

14,381 views Oct 28, 2011, 12:11pm

IBM CEO Virginia Rometty's New Leader's 100-Day Action Plan

Image by Fortune Live Media via Flickr

On the one hand, Virginia Rometty's transition into the CEO role at IBM should be relatively easy. The company is in good shape. She's been there 30 years, knows everyone, and is getting the job *because she deserves it,* as her predecessor Sam Palmisano put it.

On the other hand, these transitions are never simple.

Rometty needs to keep three things in mind as she puts together and implements her New Leader's 100-Day Action Plan:

1. The basics always apply;
2. Things are different when you get promoted from within;
3. She should consider adjusting her team's and the organization's attitude.

The Basics Always Apply

Anyone's transition into a new leadership role will go smoother if they get a head start, manage their message, and invest in building their team. These are the basics of *The New Leader's Playbook*.

Rometty has the opportunity to execute the same three-stage transition that Ajay Banga did so successfully right down the street at MasterCard.

1. She has two months left in her new role with Sam Palmisano still holding the reins as CEO.
2. She'll have a period of time as CEO and Palmisano around as Chairman.
3. She'll be in place without Palmisano around.

Rometty must take advantage of the time before her January 1 start date to jumpstart her new relationships. After 30 years in the company, she knows a ,lot of people. But no one knows her as CEO. It's a whole new game, and it's worth reconnecting with people she knows and meeting new people over the next couple of months.

Things Are Different When You Get Promoted From Within

Larry Page faced a similar situation when he got promoted from within. Our prescription is the same. Rometty needs to keep in mind she cannot control the context, cannot make a clean break and has no honeymoon.

Like Page, Rometty should prepare in advance, especially making sure to secure the resources and support she'll need going forward. She should take control of her own transition, especially around deciding what to keep the same and what to change. She should accelerate the team's progress after her start by evolving the strategies first, and then operations and organization.

Attitude Adjustment

Leadership is about inspiring and enabling others to do their absolute best, together, to realize a meaningful and rewarding shared purpose. The strongest leaders take a BRAVE approach across Behaviors, Relationships, Attitudes, Values and Environment. New leaders need to assess these dimensions and quickly figure out how to converge and evolve into the organization.

In Rometty's case, she's already inside. So, it's all about evolving. Further, it's likely she's going to be comfortable with the way the team behaves, its values and environment, and with her relationships with most team members. Inevitably there will be some team members that are detractors. She will have to identify them — especially the covert detractors (but that's a different issue).

If she is comfortable with all of these, her highest leverage point may be an attitude adjustment. Organizations' and teams' attitude or posture must line up with their strategies. Comedy troop Second City's playful, improvisational approach would be no more appropriate for GE than would be this disciplined, methodical organization's approach be appropriate for Second City. Even if Rometty and her team choose to stick with the same strategies, behaviors, relationships, and values in the environment they face, they can still up their performance by adjusting their attitude and posture in one way or another. This should be a major part of the discussion as Rometty and her team agree on their new imperative early on in her tenure.

This is a good example of step 6 of _The New Leader's Playbook_: **Embed a Strong Burning Imperative**

The burning imperative is a sharply defined, intensely shared, and purposefully urgent understanding from each of the team members of what they are "supposed to do, now." Get this created and bought into early on—even if it's only 90 percent right. You, and the team, will adjust and improve along the way.

23,821 views Nov 2, 2011, 05:44am

The Five Most Important Questions for BRAVE Leaders

BRAVE

Anyone who thinks the next 100 days are going to be anything like the last 100 days is in for a surprise. This is why we're all new leaders all the time and must continually inspire and enable others to do their absolute best, together, to realize a meaningful and rewarding shared purpose, leveraging five questions across Behaviors, Relationships, Attitudes, Values, and Environment (BRAVE leadership) from the outside in:

1. Where to play? (Environment - context)
2. What matters and why? (Values - purpose)
3. How to win? (Attitude - strategy)
4. How to connect? (Relationships - communication)
5. What impact? (Behaviors - implementation)

[Request an executive summary of our book The New Leader's 100-Day Action Plan which goes into more depth on BRAVE leadership.]

ENVIRONMENT

Today In: Leadership

One of the most important choices you make as a leader is deciding where and when to accept a position, and many do not conduct the appropriate due-diligence before accepting an offer. Zappos' Tony Hsieh likened this process to playing at a poker tournament. According to Hsieh, *"My big 'ah-ha!' moment came when I finally learned that the game started even before I sat down in a seat."*

As a leader, you must understand the context in which you're operating and interpret and create context for others. Start with your organization's history including the founders' intent. Then understand your current situation and recent results. Add to that thinking about possible future scenarios for your business and competitive conditions to inform your where to play choices.

VALUES

CEO Connection has been running CEO "Boot Camps" since 2005.
Virtually every long-serving CEO who has addressed the group agree that
the number one job of a CEO is to own and drive the company's vision
and values. Remember, happiness is good. For most people this involves a
combination of doing good for others, doing good for themselves and
doing things they are good at.

It is imperative for you as a leader to define the value you will create and
the principles you will follow to get there. A critical piece of this is moving
from theoretically elegant values that no one really believes to guiding
principles actually guiding what people do.

ATTITUDE

Strategy is about choices. You must decide how you are going to win,
where you are going to focus your efforts, and where you are *not* going to
focus. Domination over time requires a long-term view and ongoing
discipline. Success in a niche like Tony McDowell and Finch Paper requires
flexibility. Innovating like Steve Jobs and Apple requires a relentless
passion to keep one step ahead of everyone – on a continual basis.

Start with your overarching strategic posture so everyone understands
which part of Porter's value chain you're going to hang your hat on (Design
- Produce - Sell - Deliver - Support.) Then agree sub-strategies so people
know where to invest to be best-in-class, world class, strong or just good
enough. Make sure those are linked to your fundamental culture choices.

RELATIONSHIPS

Everything you do or don't say, act on, listen to and observe
communicates, 24/7, forever. You can choose a single, simplifying message
purposefully and leverage it in all your communication, strengthening
relationships along the way. Or you can let people interpret and
misinterpret things as they see fit.

Indirect communication is probably sufficient to make those complying
follow policies. If you want people to contribute, you'll need to direct
communication and guidelines. And if you want people to commit to the
cause, you must connect with them emotionally and give them the freedom
to co-create your future in line with your guiding principles.

BEHAVIORS

Environment, values, attitude and relationships all inform behaviors. Like P&G's John Pepper, you lead with your feet, with what you do, more than with what you say.

Leaders are defined by their followers. The only way to achieve your vision, in line with your values, in the context you choose, is through the attitude, relationships, and behaviors you model and engender in your followers. It's not about you. It's about your cause. Be BRAVE yourself and help them be BRAVE individually and together in a winning BRAVE culture.

4,297 views Nov 9, 2011, 07:01am

When to Lead, Follow, or Get Out of the Way: Leadership Lessons from the Greek Bailout

Image via Wikipedia

Greek Prime Minister George Papandreou is choosing to get out of the way and resign in order to save the bailout deal for his country. Sometimes leaders need to lead. Sometimes they need to follow. And sometimes they need to get out of the way of the pursuit of purpose.

Whenever a leader is facing a period of change, there are going to be supporters, detractors and watchers:

- **Supporters:** These are the people that share the leader's vision and see that there's more to gain by going forward with the new leader than by holding on to the past.

- **Detractors:** These are the people who are comfortable with the status quo and have more to lose in giving up the current state than they have to gain in supporting a risky change.

- **Watchers:** These are the people that are on the fence, generally the silent majority.

It is difficult to turn detractors into supporters (especially covert detractors). Instead, leaders should work to turn supporters into champions, watchers into supporters, and neutralize detractors, turning them into watchers or making them go away.

Ideal Result

The ideal result for Papandreou would have been to align the government leaders around the shared purpose of improving the well-being of the people of Greece. He could not do this, so he tried to move enough of his supporters, watchers, and detractors one step each to alter the balance of power in his favor.

Papandreou tried, but was unable to shift enough people to save the deal. If you can't do that as a leader, it's time to get out of the way, like Papandreou did to pave the way for what Lucas Papedemos must do as interim prime minister.

The Win

One of the issues with the Greek bailout was that some of the people did not want to give Papandreou the win, fearing that it would strengthen his hold on the government. He tried all sorts of approaches, from encouragement to bargaining to threats to calling a public referendum. None worked.

So, in the end, Papandreou agreed to give up his position, taking off the table any risk of a win strengthening his hold.

Commit to Purpose

The strongest leaders know that it's not about them. It's about the team, their followers, and, most importantly, the purpose of the organization (improving the wellbeing of the people of Greece in this case). Papandreou's action is the action of a leader more committed to purpose than to his own "hold" on power.

The lesson is most definitely not that any leader facing opposition should resign. The lesson is that leaders must be committed to purpose over everything else. Had Papandreou managed to get the other governmental leaders rallied around their shared purpose and put their disagreements aside in pursuit of that, he would not have had to resign. He failed in that. And that failure is a failure of leadership.

The risk is that those that dug in and forced Papandreou's resignation will be emboldened by their success and be even less flexible in the future. Papandreou certainly knows that. The choice he is making is to accept that risk - but do the deal required for the bailout.

This is a good example of step 9 of _The New Leader's Playbook_: **Secure ADEPT People in the Right Roles and Deal with Inevitable Resistance**

Make your organization ever more ADEPT by Acquiring, Developing, Encouraging, Planning, and Transitioning talent:

- **Acquire**: Recruit, attract, and onboard the right people
- **Develop**: Assess and build skills and knowledge
- **Encourage**: Direct, support, recognize, and reward
- **Plan**: Monitor, assess, plan career moves over time
- **Transition**: Migrate to different roles as appropriate

Just as not all people are right for all roles, not all leaders are right for all situations. We're all new leaders all the time. As you take a look at your next 100 days, make sure you know when to lead, when to follow, and when to get out of the way.

1,221 views Nov 10, 2011, 07:49am

What Greece's Interim Prime Minister Lucas Papademos Must Do

Image by AFP/Getty Images via @daylife

Managing an interim assignment is one of the most challenging things any leader ever does under any circumstances, let alone when your charge is on the verge of defaulting, scuttling the EU, and "putting a dent" in the world economy in a bad way. What then is Lucas Papademos to do as Greece's interim prime minister?

We address interim assignments in our book, *The New Leader's 100-Day Action Plan*, and suggest that interim leaders must start by getting clarity on whether *interim* means "*holding the fort until we find the right person, which absolutely will not be you, on probation with a good chance of becoming permanent, or doing the job as a developmental opportunity on the way to something else.*"

In this case, it seems clear that interim means "*getting us through the crisis of approving the bailout and then going away so the real politicians can get back to running the country.*" This means Papademos should treat this more like a discrete, temporary assignment with no expectations of a continuing role.

The need for bad guys

In a lot of cases, organizations need "bad guys" to make them take their medicine. Almost by definition, turnarounds are not fun. A lot of the practices and habits of the past need to be jettisoned to make way for a new set of actions that will allow the organization to reverse course. In the most extreme cases, organizations need to rethink all the BRAVE components of their culture (Behaviors, Relationships, Attitudes, Values, Environment).

People don't like change. And by association, they may not like the leader that's forcing the change upon them. This is why so many leaders of turnarounds have such short tenures in organizations. They come in, do exactly what they were asked to do, and are then jettisoned once they've completed their task.

This is why we suggest leaders of turnarounds bring in their own fall guys. Instead of taking the blame themselves, these leaders bring in interim leaders or outside consultants to manage the turnaround efforts. Once the turnarounds are set, they affix all the blame for all the pain on the interim project managers, make them go away, and ask the organization to follow them to a brighter future. They make others be the bad guys so they can be the good guys.

Greek bad guy

In many respects, this is what's going on in Greece. Neither the current government, nor the opposition thinks it can carry through the deal and its austerity measures without being forever perceived as the "bad guys." Instead, Papandreou is getting out of the way and putting Papademos and his government into the "bad guy" position, hopefully setting themselves up to be the good guys afterwards.

It's not clear this is going to work in Greece. But it will work in many of your organizations.

What Papademos should do

The basics of onboarding into a new role always apply. A little discipline goes a long way. Papedemos can improve his chances of success by getting a head start, managing the message and building the team – even in an interim assignment. He should:

- Get a head start by making sure the coalition is committed to what it's telling him to do.
- Manage the message with all the critical stakeholders including the coalition, EU leaders, and Greek populace as a whole.
- Build the team – even for the interim. This team is going to ramp up, complete its task and go away. None of that makes its ability to function as a high-performing team any less important.

This is a good example of step 1 of *The New Leader's Playbook*: **Position Yourself for Success**

There are several components of this including positioning yourself for a leadership role, selling before you buy, mapping and avoiding the most common land mines, uncovering hidden risks in the organization, role, and fit, and choosing the right approach for your transition type.

In some cases, you position yourself for success by letting someone else go into the role first so they can fail and you can come in as the savior. Sometimes necessary. Often effective.

17,428 views Nov 16, 2011, 12:10pm

Five Keys to Managing an Unpredictable Boss

Image via Wikipedia

Wouldn't it be nice if management theory actually worked in practice? Wouldn't it be nice if you could follow the tenets of The New Leader's 100-Day Action Plan to get your strategic, operating, and organizational processes in place and let them run without interruption? Wouldn't it be nice if your boss had perfect leadership skills and gave you clear direction and then never changed his or her mind?

Welcome to the real world. The real world is messy. Things change. And we all must adapt to those changes on an ongoing basis.

Brilliant Bosses are Mercurial

The most brilliant entrepreneurs, leaders and bosses change their minds. They pride themselves on zigging while others zag. They don't care about the process. They are passionately focused on a vision. They are relentless in pursuing what's important. They will change anything at any time, except their core values, to reach their end goal.

This is why people like <u>Steve Jobs</u> throw out less than perfect prototypes. This is why other brilliant entrepreneurs are sometimes hard to work with.

I just got back from two weeks in China, Malaysia, Singapore and India. I met a handful of entrepreneurs and the people working for them. The various conversations I had with people doing better or worse in managing mercurial bosses led me to consider the five ways to manage an unpredictable or volatile boss.

Five BRAVE Keys

The five keys to managing a mercurial boss are the same as the five keys to managing any boss and culture: <u>Behaviors, Relationships, Attitudes, Values, Environment</u>.

Behaviors

Behave with integrity. What you do must match what you say and what you fundamentally believe. Integrity does not mean blind consistency. It's fine for you to change direction in response to changing circumstances. You just have to let those following you know why. When your boss changes his or her mind based on something he or she sees that others don't see, step in to explain that to others.

Relationships

In a business setting, the relationship between a boss and subordinate is of primary importance. If you're working for a mercurial boss, you need to align the mode, manner, and frequency of your communication with what your boss prefers. And you need to disagree with them in the right way. Different people prefer being disagreed with in different ways, ranging from:

- Never disagree with me
- Challenge me one-on-one, but only in private
- Challenge me in team meetings, but never let anyone outside "the family" know what you're thinking
- Challenge me in public – but politely.
- Gloves off, all the time, because public challenges communicate the culture we want

You cannot survive a mercurial boss without knowing how to do this –
and adapting as your boss changes.

Attitudes

You have to believe in your boss. Mercurial changes viewed through an
attitude of belief and respect look very different than they do through an
attitude of doubt. Choose the right attitude and approach.

Values

We've had a series of amazing legacy CEOs come to <u>CEO Connection
CEO Boot Camps</u> to share their perspective on what's worked and not
worked in their careers. Virtually every one of them says that the
fundamental job of the CEO is to own the vision and the values. Got to
have the vision. Got to move things towards that vision whatever it takes –
except for compromising your values. If you believe the end justifies the
means, you will not be the same person when you get there.

Thus, if you have a mercurial boss, make sure your values are completely in
line with his or hers. If you share the same values, the tactical changes are
far easier to handle.

Environment

Context counts. The physical environment makes a difference. The way
you organize and decorate your offices makes a difference. The way you
dress makes a difference.

One middle manager's office is perfectly designed to make the people
working for him respect him while, at the same time, never making his
boss feel that the middle manager is trying to compete with him. This
manager's office, like the way he dresses, behaves, and relates to others,
have found that happy middle way.

This is a good example of step 10 of *The New Leader's Playbook*: **Evolve
People, Plans, and Practices to Capitalize on Changing
Circumstances**

By the end of your first 100-Days, you should have made significant steps
toward aligning your people, plans, and practices around a shared purpose.

Remember, this is not a one-time event but, instead, something that will require constant, ongoing management and Darwinian improvement.

I thought about saying this was a good example of positioning yourself for success – which, of course, it is if you're going into a new role. But it's not a one-time thing with brilliant, mercurial bosses. As they evolve, you must evolve with them.

3,158 views Nov 22, 2011, 10:01am

How John Smale Changed the Business Environment for Procter & Gamble

Image by R.B. Boyer via Flickr

In the pantheon of signs, symbol, and stories that help people understand Procter & Gamble's (P&G) culture, one of the classics is how former P&G CEO John Smale got the American Dental Association (ADA) to change its approach to approving products and endorse Crest toothpaste, and then leveraged that endorsement to triple Crest's market share.

Two of the fundamental pillars of a creative brief are benefit (the promise) and support (the reason to believe). In the 1950s, the main benefit of toothpaste was to prevent cavities - as it had been since fluoride was first added to toothpaste in 1914. There was relatively little differentiation between the top toothpastes on either benefit or support.

Smale saw an opportunity to differentiate through an expert endorsement - in this case, the ADA's. The ADA had never endorsed a product, but P&G had developed a safer fluoride. So Smale went to work convincing them. It took literally years of effort including attending ADA meetings on his own time. But when he got the ADA's endorsement and layered that on to Crest's "Look Mom, no cavities" advertising campaign, Crest's market share tripled and it became the market leader.

The story is told over and over again at P&G (and I suspect later at General Motors when Smale pulled it back from the brink of bankruptcy and restored it to profitability as its chairman, and also at J.P. Morgan and Eastman Kodak where he served on their boards) as an example of:

- The power of differentiation
- Different ways to differentiate
- Overcoming barriers
- Consumer focus
- Taking a long-term view

Crest went on to continued success behind other innovations. Smale, who died on Nov. 19, went on to become one of P&G's most respected CEOs ever, serving as a great model for each aspect of BRAVE leadership: Behaviors, Relationships, Attitude, Values and Environment.

Behaviors

The ADA Crest endorsement is a prime example. Other examples include his willingness to work long hours, make the big bets on acquisitions, and face problems head on like P&G's supply chain and approach to working with customers. I worked at P&G in marketing during the time Smale was CEO, and remember in particular his uncanny ability to ask the one question that got at the heart of the matter. Former P&G CEO John Pepper said this of Smale to Reuters:

John was the single most inspiring leader I have ever known. Period.

Relationships

Smale was disciplined and driven, but always made time to make others feel important.

I remember John's compassion best. He had the uncanny ability to make you feel like he was listening with an open mind to everything you said. I first met John as a brand assistant and felt it was remarkable a man in his position would care so much about what I had to say. It was inspirational and made me feel like a true owner of the business. — Ed Burghard, former P&G marketing manager

Attitude

Smale was relentlessly focused on doing good over the long term.

He put the long-term strength of his organization ahead of the short-term impact of tough choices. And he embodied a commitment to improve the lives of our consumers in small

and large ways and to have a positive impact on society. – Jim Stengel, former P&G CMO, in <u>Advertising Age April 1, 2002</u>

Values

You can stop anybody at P&G dead in their tracks by asking "Are you sure we're doing the right thing?" Smale embodied the right thing.

I will remember John most for his character, how he represented the soul of the company: purpose-inspired, caring yet demanding, principled and humble. – Bob McDonald, current P&G CEO, in <u>Cincinnati</u>.com November 19, 2011

Environment

Smale was one of the great change agents, inspiring and enabling others from within. This was deep-seeded in Smale, as one of his early jobs was to gather petitions to help Cincinnati's NuMaid Margarine change an archaic law prohibiting margarine from being yellow. The lesson he learned was to change laws, regulations and polices that inhibit progress. Not only can you choose where to play, but you can change your environment over time.

The one thing that distinguishes John's career as the leader of our company has been his remarkable record as an agent for change. – Ed Artzt, former P&G CEO, in <u>Cincinnati.com, November 19, 2011</u>

This is a good example of step 2 of *The New Leader's Playbook*: **Engage the Culture and Your New Colleagues in the Right Context**

Be careful about how you engage with the organization's existing business context and culture. Crossing the need for change based on the context and the cultural readiness for change can help you decide whether to Assimilate, Converge and Evolve (fast or slow), or Shock.

Perhaps what was so remarkable about Smale was that he changed both P&G's internal culture and external context for the better over the long term.

1,334 views Nov 30, 2011, 10:16am

How Merkel Can Lead the Euro Zone Out of Crisis

This is the moment for German Chancellor Angela Merkel to choose to take up the mantle of European leadership ...or not.

It must be tempting for her to let things unfold as they might for the rest of Europe. She knows that many of the other 16 members of the euro zone are enduring and will endure a great deal of pain. And staying out of the fray is a way to delay pain in Germany.

But the euro zone's pain will be Germany's pain eventually. And it's looking more and more like the later people take their medicine, the worse the pain will be in the end. A system built on a common currency without a corresponding common fiscal policy and tools is as untenable as four people driving a single car in which each person has their own steering wheel, attached to their own one of the four tires, trying to steer their own route.

The only long-term solution is to fix the system. Over the short term, it may be possible to coordinate actions across the different parties to increase liquidity, but over time, monetary and fiscal efforts must be aligned. The euro zone must either sever the monetary piece and go back to separate currencies or merge the fiscal piece.

So easy to say. So hard to do.

Everybody has an opinion. Some have multiple opinions. Reuters' top two headlines yesterday morning were:

1) "Stock Futures Gain on Relief Over Italy Bond Auction"

and

2) "Italy Borrowing Costs Soar as Euro Pressure Mounts"

You can't make up this stuff. Was Italy's bond auction good news or bad news or both?

Back to Merkel. She has three options:

1. Focus on Germany's fiscal efforts. Keep Germany strong and out of the fray as much as possible.
2. Let the common currency collapse.
3. Use this crisis as a way to push through a euro zone fiscal union.

There are pros and cons to each.

Staying out of the fray

This is akin to the man on the deck of the Titanic who turns to his companion and says, "I'm glad the hole is not on our side of the boat." Germany can stay out of the fray only so long. When Europe goes down, Germany will go down with it.

Letting the currency collapse

Chuck Forgang likes to say the contract side of his law practice is like scrambling and unscrambling eggs. He goes on to note that the scrambling is far easier than the unscrambling. Unscrambling the euro-denominated contracts will not be pretty. And, when the currencies are separated, it's likely that some, like Germany's, will go way up, choking their exports, and others will go way down, bankrupting a lot of people. None of this will be good for Germany.

Fiscal union

The pain associated with transitioning to a fiscal union will be high. Many citizens will think giving up more control to a central system that has proved it doesn't work is completely irrational. It is, however, the only option that has viability after the pain.

The time has come for Europe to take its medicine. Merkel is the only one in a position to make it happen. Let's all hope she does.

This is a good example of step 5 of <u>The New Leader's Playbook</u>, Embed a Burning Imperative.

The burning imperative is a sharply defined, intensely shared, and purposefully urgent understanding from each of the team members of what they are supposed to do, now.

For the euro zone leaders, the key is to make *purposefully urgent choices.*

Purposefully

They must start by being clear on their purpose. In theory, the euro zone was created because the well-being of the people of each individual nation would be enhanced by bonding together. If the leaders keep that purpose in mind, they will work through the short-term distractions on the way together. If they don't keep that in mind, they will likely end up going their separate ways.

Urgent

The clock is running down. The acceleration of news, events, downgrades and the like means that the leaders must make their choices with great urgency.

Choices

They must make real choices. As discussed above, their choices are going to have significant consequences and are not going to be easy. But as they weigh the different impacts on different people, they must keep in mind that choosing not to choose is itself a choice - and one with all sorts of unintended consequences.

37,687 views Dec 7, 2011, 07:12am

Lessons from The Animal School Fable in Leveraging Strengths

An adaptation of George Reavis' fable, "The Animal School", originally written in 1940, when he was superintendent of the Cincinnati Public Schools.

"The Animal School" Fable: An Adaptation

The animals organized a school to help their children deal with the problems of the new world. And to make it easier to administer the curriculum of running, climbing, swimming and flying, they decided that all their children would take all the subjects. This produced some interesting issues.

The duck was excellent in swimming but relatively poor in running, so he devoted himself to improving his running through extra practice. Eventually, his webbed feet got so badly worn that he dropped to only average in swimming. But average was acceptable in this school so nobody worried about that, except the duck.

The rabbit had a nervous breakdown because the other animals said she looked like a rat when she jumped in the water for swimming class and all her hair got matted down.

In the climbing class, the eagle beat all the others to the top of the tree, but kept insisting on using his own method of getting there. This was unacceptable, so the eagle was severely disciplined.

And then the fish came home from school and said, *"Mom, Dad, I hate school. Swimming is great. Flying is fun if they let me start in the water. But running and climbing? I don't have any legs; and I can't breathe out of the water."*

The fish's parents made an appointment for her with the principal who took one look at her progress reports and decreed, *"You are so far ahead of the rest of the class in swimming that we're going to let you skip swimming classes and give you private tutoring in running and climbing."*

The fish was last seen heading for Canada to request political asylum. The moral of this story is:

Let the fish swim. Let the rabbits run. Let the eagles fly.

We don't want a school of average ducks.

or, **Play to people's strengths.**

Investing in Strengths

It's a lesson we learn over and over again. Most of us are unbalanced. We are relatively stronger in one area than another. There is a great temptation to fix ourselves or others by investing time to improve the areas that are relatively less strong. But that's not the way forward.

The better approach is to invest time to improve the areas that are already relatively strong, and find ways to compensate for the gaps. That could be leveraging technology or partnering with someone else. If you are relatively weak at managing operational details, partner with a strong chief operating officer. If you are relatively weak at dealing with people's problems and issues, partner with a strong chief human resource officer. If you are relatively weak at coming up with strategies, partner with a strong chief strategy officer.

This is why our firm just announced new alliances in China and India. Instead of trying to be all things to all people, we're going to be the best we can be at one thing, executive onboarding and transition acceleration, and partner with others with complementary strengths and local knowledge.

This is a good example of step 9 of _The New Leader's Playbook_: **Secure ADEPT People in the Right Roles and Deal with Inevitable Resistance**

Make your organization ever more ADEPT by Acquiring, Developing, Encouraging, Planning, and Transitioning talent:

- **Acquire**: Recruit, attract, and onboard the right people
- **Develop**: Assess and build skills and knowledge
- **Encourage**: Direct, support, recognize, and reward
- **Plan**: Monitor, assess, plan career moves over time
- **Transition**: Migrate to different roles as appropriate

240 views Dec 12, 2011, 07:38am

Follow the Money to Understand Last Week's European Summit

Crises change things. The difference between managing a crisis and leading through one is often related to leaders' ability to keep their eyes on what really matters. One of the lessons from last week's European debt crisis summit is how difficult it is to manage across groups when what really matters is different for each player.

Germany

Germany's leader Merkel, was the only one who could lead the group through the crisis. From the German paper, Handelsblatt's and The New York Times' perspective, it was Merkel's vision and master plan that prevailed.

"Der Masterplan gegen die Eurokrise" (Germany's Handelsblatt – "The Master Plan Against the Crisis")

"German Vision Prevails as Leaders Agree on Fiscal Pact" (The New York Times)

France

France's leader, Sarkozy, was scared. France's banks were, and are, at risk. He needed some progress and is hoping the worst is over. (We'll see.)

"Crise de la zone euro : et si le pire était passé?" (France's Le Monde – "The worst is over")

United Kingdom

The U.K. did not want to get sucked into the euro death spiral. It was feeling pretty good that it had kept its own currency and neither wanted to, nor felt that it needed to, give up its fiscal sovereignty.

"Britain stands alone" (The Times of London)

"Britain's cold shoulder for Europe" (Financial Times – U.K.)

European Union

While much is left to be decided, it does look like there is some sort of split coming.

"Europe's great divorce" (Economist)

"Questions Plague EU Fiscal Pact" (The Wall Street Journal)

Leading Through a Crisis

In a crisis, it's important to keep the ultimate purpose in mind. That purpose needs to inform and frame everything you do over the short-, mid-, and long-term as you lead *through* a crisis instead of merely *out* of a crisis. Crises change your organization. Be sure that the choices you make during crises change you in ways that move you toward your purpose and not away from your core vision and values. (From "The New Leader's 100-Day Action Plan." For a white paper on leading through a crisis, click here.)

Follow the Money

In the case of the euro crisis, it's reasonable to assume that each leader was looking out for the well being of his or her own country's citizens. It's not surprising that Merkel and Sarkozy were more closely aligned in their approach while the U.K.'s Cameron was not. Germany and France share the same currency. The U.K. does not. Over time, it has become more and more clear that monetary alignment does not work without fiscal alignment. Without the pull of the monetary union, it's not surprising that the U.K. balked at a closer fiscal union.

Leading Different Groups Through a Crisis Together

Leading different groups through a crisis together requires a shared purpose. You must find the common ground across different groups to have a hope of getting people aligned around a common approach. This could be a common, shared goal. Or it could be a common, shared desire to do good for someone else.

This is a good example of step 6 of _The New Leader's Playbook_: **Embed a Strong Burning Imperative**

The burning imperative is a sharply defined, intensely shared, and purposefully urgent understanding from each of the team members of what they are "supposed to do, now." Get this created and bought into early on—even if it's only 90 percent right. You, and the team, will adjust and improve along the way.

The learning from the European debt crisis is just how important it is to figure out what matters to each of the different parties involved. The more they share a common purpose, the easier it is going to be to get them to share an imperative.

1,280 views Dec 19, 2011, 01:11pm

Kim Jong Un's Challenges in Taking Over the Family Business (North Korea)

Taking over the business from the family patriarch or matriarch is challenging. Especially if the previous head was more autocratic than empowering. Especially if the new leader has not had time to prove himself or herself. Especially if the change is sudden. Especially if the business is in trouble. Especially if the family business is a country. So, it's fair to assume that Kim Jong Un will face some challenges in taking over Kim Jong II's place.

Others will comment on whether or not it is in anyone's best interest for Kim Jong Un to be successful. I'm going to focus on his transition as an acid test of dealing with supporters, detractors and watchers.

Supporters are the people that share your vision and see that there's more to gain by going forward with the new leader than by holding on to the past. Detractors are the people who are comfortable with the status quo and think they have more to lose in giving up the current state than they have to gain in supporting a risky change. Watchers are the people that are on the fence, generally the silent majority.

They are always there in a leadership transition and their influence is even more complex in a transition within a family business. It's never easy to turn detractors into supporters. Trying to do so is the wrong approach. A better approach is to move everyone one step. Turn the detractors into watchers or get them out of the way. Turn some of the watchers into supporters. Turn some of the supporters into champions. If a leader can do that, the balance of power shifts and progress is made.

Supporters

Start here. This is a pull strategy, not a push strategy. Find the most willing and able supporters and enroll them. Give them more responsibility. Give them more status. Give them projects they can move forward. Set them up as beacons of success for others to follow. These will be the most rewarding moves you can make – for them, for you, for everyone. Invest in your strengths. Feed what's working.

I have no idea who Kim Jong Un's real supporters are. The problem is that Kim Jong Un probably doesn't either. There will be many that proclaim their support. There will be some that mean it. His chances of success will be greatly enhanced if he can tell the difference. Additionally, he should reach outside of the most accessible circle to find other people that will support him and bring them closer to him. He needs real allies – badly.

Detractors

Every single legacy, long-serving CEO that has addressed CEO Connection's CEO Boot Camps since 2005 has said in one way or another that he or she wishes she had moved faster on the people. This is an even bigger issue in a family business because of all the family ties. It's not just the people with the same last name. It's the people that married into the family. It's the friends of the family. It's the loyal supporters of the family. Family businesses tend to reward loyalty and close ties. And all sorts of people have all sorts of back channel ways of getting their message to the people with real power – whether or not they actually show up in the office.

But a new leader must neutralize the overt and covert detractors before they undo him or her. Some can be persuaded to give the new leader a chance to prove himself or herself. Some can be moved to positions where they can do less damage. Some need to go away. It is critical to time these moves right. Too fast and the other detractors will gang up on the new leader. Too slow and things will get out of control.

The odds are that Kim Jong Un will move very decisively on his detractors. We may never know how he makes them go away. We will know if he doesn't move fast enough. And we'll know that very soon.

Watchers

Not all watchers are the same. Some watchers are leaning towards becoming supporters. Some are leaning towards becoming detractors. All will be influenced by what they see. Hence the term "watchers."

The key here is to identify the watchers you can't see. In a family business this includes all the people behind the scenes like lawyers, accountants, bankers – both those serving the business and those serving family members.

You must identify them. You must track them. You must know how they move. If more switch to supporters over time, you win. If more switch to detractors over time, you lose.

There is an international community watching Kim Jong Un. A large piece of how successful he is going to be depends on how the people watching from China feel. Again, I suspect we'll learn about that relatively soon.

Advice for people taking over family businesses (that aren't countries)

It's important to map and move the stakeholders one step at a time in any new leadership role:

-     turn supporters into champions

-     turn watchers into supporters

-     turn detractors into watchers or get them out of the way

In taking over a family business, you must map beyond what you can easily see and choose your timing very carefully.

A 28-year-old with almost no experience suddenly taking over a country in desperate trouble that's been run by a despot has no margin for error.

This is a good example of step 2 of _The New Leader's Playbook_: **Engage the Culture and Your New Colleagues in the Right** Context

Be careful about how you engage with the organization's existing business context and culture. Crossing the need for change based on the context and the cultural readiness for change can help you decide whether to Assimilate, Converge and Evolve (fast or slow), or Shock.

If Kim Jong Un doesn't get this right, the rest of the steps are irrelevant.

2,427 views Dec 21, 2011, 06:43am

Leading by Example with Flames of Giving

We're all leaders all the time. Everything we do, everything we say, everything we don't do and don't say communicates. We lead with our examples. Sari Gross's Flames of Giving program is a classic case of leading by example.

Almost two decades ago, Sari was looking for ways to make her children more aware of, and more connected with, the community around them. She knew there were others in need. She wanted her children to understand *"that people in need are everywhere and you can do something to make a difference."*

So she called some local agencies that connected her and her children with people in need. They wrote up "little flames" with information about the people in need and recruited their friends and neighbors to donate gifts. That year, they collected and distributed 40 gifts.

The next year, her children asked if they could do it again. And a movement began.

Now, 17 years later, people that Sari and her children don't know call her and ask *"When is the flames program starting. I want to go shopping."* This year they will give away approximately 1,000 gifts. The program takes over Sari's life (and her house) from October to December.

This is a serious, big time model that anyone can follow. Sari is clear on the basics:

Connecting with people

Although all the donors and recipients remain anonymous, each "flame,"

Describes a specific person in a way that people can attach their heart to.

Go back and read what the Red Cross's <u>Charley Shimanski</u> says about connecting with his team. He doesn't think about what he's going to say. He doesn't think about what they're going to hear. He thinks about how they are going to feel. This is the same thing. The gift is a medium for connecting two hearts.

Connecting with other human beings is important for all involved. We connect in different ways: through personal contact, through visuals, through words. Sari's Flames of Giving connects people that don't know each other through gifts.

Take the first step

As Sari puts it,

The only thing I've ever seen make a difference is one person or a group of people getting together and taking their idea off the piece of paper and getting out there and moving it forward.

Ideas are useless. It's behaviors that make an impact. Sari put her idea into action, first with just her children. Then with other neighbors and agencies to help find people in need.

Give up control to multiply the impact

Sari is not completely in control of what's happening, which is fine because she is convinced that, *"Things happen for a reason."* Now gifts arrive at her doorstep and people arrive at her door and she has no idea where they came from.

Sari is not sure where to take this next. She wants to spend some time thinking about it.

I'm hoping something will come to me and I'll be brave enough to go for it.

She thinks it may be helping others start similar programs in other parts of the country and the world.

People are hesitant to do things on their own, but if I give them a little bit of guidance or structure, they take it and run with it. I may need to pull myself out of the process and pull them into it.

Lessons for other leaders

Which other leaders? All of us. And this means you. You have ideas. You have thoughts about things that could make stronger connections between the people in your organization. You have ideas that can connect people in your community. What's holding you back?

- Focus your efforts on connecting people.
- Get your ideas out of your head, off the piece of paper, and get started.
- Give others guidance and structure, and let them take it and run with it to multiply your impact.

If you need help, send Sari Gross an email at SSLB28@aol.com. She'd be delighted to share her experience as an example for you to follow.

This is a good example of step 8 of *The New Leader's Playbook*: **Over-invest in Early Wins to Build Team Confidence**

Early wins are all about credibility and confidence. People have more faith in people who have delivered. You want your boss to have confidence in you. You want team members to have confidence in you, in themselves, and in the plan for change that has emerged. Early wins fuel that confidence.

This was never about Sari. It started as a way to model behavior for her children. It's become a model of good behavior for her community. Sari's hope is that others flame the spark of this idea in other communities.

6,879 views Dec 28, 2011, 07:47am

Leadership Lessons from the World's Top Companies: 2011 Year in Review

BRAVE

Happy New Year! As you undertake a new job or assignment in 2012, keep in mind the three steps which will help you succeed in a new job or initiative:

1. Get a head start.
2. Manage the message.
3. Build the team.

I looked back at the articles I've written over the past 11 months and picked a few that convey best practices for each step. They should help make your coming year happier. Click through to the original articles for more.

Get a Head Start

A new job doesn't start on day one. It starts during the interview. See "Top Executive Recruiters Agree There Are Only Three True Job Interview Questions" for tips on how to discover during the interview if you'll enjoy working for the company.

Should you receive the job offer, take cues from Zappos' Tony Hsieh to discover the "Three Key Onboarding Due Diligence Questions" which will help you gauge the level of risk associated with the new role, and whether you should accept the offer.

After accepting an offer, but before day one, get a pulse on the corporate culture of the organization by taking a BRAVE approach: examine its behaviors, relationships, attitudes, values and environment. See "Will Robert Gibbs Find a Friend in Facebook?" for a framework to analyze corporate culture.

If you are promoted to a new leadership role from within a company, you will face unique challenges. See "Promoted From Within -- Thoughts For Google's New CEO Larry Page" for tips on how to approach the situation differently than if you were hired from outside the organization.

Manage the Message

Day one in a new job is key. Everything is magnified and everything communicates, whether you want it to or not. Read about "Meg Whitman's Day One Itinerary as CEO of Hewlett-Packard" for some do's and don'ts of day one behavior.

Driving a message as a leader is difficult, but you can take cues from the late Steve Jobs about the power of a focused message – "Steve Jobs and the Power of a Passionate Focus."

Crafting a focus message is key, but keep your target audience in mind. As we saw from "JPMorgan CEO Jamie Dimon's Public Lambasting of the Bank of Canada," executives must be clear about whom they are trying to influence, and when and how to do that directly and indirectly.

Build the Team

An important team-building tool for leaders is leveraging milestones to keep projects on track and recognize employee achievements. See "Royal Caribbean's CEO Exemplifies How to Leverage Milestones."

Often, leaders must change the organization's culture as business strategies shift. See the steps True Value Hardware CEO Lyle Heidemann took to change the company's culture so that its focus could shift from its traditional wholesale excellence to retail expertise in "True Value Hardware Deploys Three Keys to Successful Culture Change."

Your work is not finished after the first 100 days. Read "GE CEO Jeff Immelt's Long-term View 10 Years In" for a perfect example of how every leader should view the first 100 days of 2012 as the first 100 days of the rest of your career.

The New Leader's Playbook

To see how a leader can implement all three steps, read "IBM CEO Virginia Rometty's New Leader's 100-Day Action Plan" or "Caryn Lerner's 100-Day Action Plan as New CEO of Daffy's."

Getting a head start, managing the message, and building the team are, of course, the framework for the ten steps of *The New Leader's Playbook*.

About the author

George Bradt has led the revolution in how people start new jobs - accelerating transitions so leaders and their teams reduce their rates of failure and fulfill potential. After Harvard and Wharton (MBA), he progressed through sales, marketing, and general management roles around the world at Unilever, Procter & Gamble, Coca-Cola, and J.D. Power's Power Information Network spin off as chief executive. Now he is a Principal of CEO Connection, Chairman of PrimeGenesis, author of seven books on onboarding and leadership, over 600 columns for Forbes, and fifteen musical plays, plays and screenplays (book, lyrics & music).

Onboarding & leadership books authored or co-authored by George Bradt:
- CEO Boot Camp (GHP Press 2019)
- Point of Inflection (GHP Press 2017-19)
- The New Leader's 100-Day Action Plan (John Wiley & Sons, 2006, 2009, 2011, 2016)
- First-Time Leader (John Wiley & Sons, 2014)
- The New Job 100-Day Plan (GHP Press, 2012)
- The Total Onboarding Program: An Integrated Approach (Wiley/Pfeiffer, 2010)
- Onboarding: How to Get Your New Employees up to Speed in Half the Time (John Wiley & Sons, 2009)

George can be reached at gbradt@primegenesis.com

www.ingramcontent.com/pod-product-compliance
Lightning Source LLC
Chambersburg PA
CBHW031113250726
48655CB00004B/1695